How to use this b[ook]

How to use this book.

Each conversation, song, rap, poem or joke is accompanied by this symbol.

This will quickly enable you to find the track required on the CDs.
The number in bold relates to the CD (1, 2 or 3).

The next number (not in bold) is the track required, e.g. **2.**2 means CD2 track 2.

1 means CD1    **2** means CD2    **3** means CD3

K means Karaoke Track, e.g. **K.1.**33 means that the karaoke version of the song or rap can be found on CD 1, track 33.

Lied   means *song*.

Volkslied   means *folksong*.

Reim   means *rhyme*.

Gespräch   means *dialogue* or *conversation*.

Witz   means *joke*.

Zungenbrecher   means *tongue-twister*.

Rap   means *song* or *poem set to a rhythm*.

Schlaflied   means *lullaby*.

Weihnachtslied   means *Christmas carol*.

WITHDRAWN

Copyright Carole Nicoll 2005

Inhalt

Contents	Page
Grüße *greetings*	1
Das Alphabet *alphabet*	3
Im Klassenzimmer *in the classroom*	5
Tiere *animals*	7
Farben *colours*	9
Tage *days*	12
Monate *months*	13
Mein Geburtstag *my birthday*	14
Jahreszeiten *seasons*	15
Das Wetter *the weather*	17
Wie siehst du aus? *What do you look like?*	21
Die Familie *the family*	23
Das Café *the café*	25
Sportarten *sports*	27
Die Zeit *the time*	29

Copyright Carole Nicoll 2005

Inhalt

	In meinem Schlafzimmer *in my bedroom*	31
	Verkehrsmittel *transport*	33
	Der Körper *the body*	37
	Die Kleidung *clothes*	41
	Die Stadt *the town*	44
	Der Zoo *the zoo*	47
	Der Bauernhof *the farm*	49
	Weihnachten *Christmas*	55
	Zahlen 1-60 *numbers 1-60*	57
	Zahlen 61-100+ *numbers 60-100+*	59
	Grammatik *grammar*	61
	CD1 Track Listings	79
	CD2 Track Listings	80
	CD3 Track Listings	81
	CD English Transcripts	82

Copyright Carole Nicoll 2005

Grüße 1

	Guten Morgen! **Guten Tag!** *Good Morning!/Good Day!*		**der Junge** *the boy*
	Guten Abend! *Good Afternoon!/ Good Evening!*		**der Freund** *the chum, friend, pal (male)*
	Gute Nacht! *Good Night!*		**Frau** *lady/Mrs/Madam*
	Hallo! *Hello!/Cheerio!*		**Fräulein** *Miss*
	Tschüss *Goodbye!*		**das Mädchen** *the girl*
	Herr *Sir/Mr*		**die Freundin** *the chum, friend, pal (female)*

Gespräch 1

Hallo, wie geht's?

Es geht mir gut, und dir?

Sehr gut, danke!

Wiedersehen, Herr Braun!

Bis später, Herr Schmidt!

Bis nächste Woche!

Gut danke

Gespräch 2

Wie geht's?

Nicht gut!

Warum?

Mein Finger tut weh!

Ach schade!

Copyright Carole Nicoll 2005

Grüße

Rap

Guten Tag! Gute Nacht!
Guten Morgen! Gute Nacht!
Guten Abend! Gute Nacht!
Wie geht's? Gar nicht schlecht!
Hallo, wie heißt du? (x 3)
Ich heiße Carla!
Auf Wiedersehen! Bis später! (x 3)
Auf Wiedersehen, Frau Schmidt!

Reim

Wie heißt du?
Ich heiße Udo.
Wie heißt er?
Er heißt Pierre.
Wie heißt sie?
Sie heißt Marie.
Danke Peter!
Bis später!

Lied
...Gute Nacht, Mädchen

Gute Nacht, Mädchen!
Tschüss, Herr Klein! (x2)
Hallo, wie geht's?
Es geht mir gut!
Gute Nacht, Mädchen!
Tschüss, Herr Klein!

Guten Tag, mein Junge.
Wie heißt du? (x2)
Ich heiße Peter.
Und er heißt Dieter!
Guten Tag, Junge.
Wie heißt du?

Schönes Wochenende und viel Spaß!
Bis nächste Woche, Frau Glas!
Gute Reise, Peter!
Tschüs und bis später!
Bis Morgen früh und tschau!

Gespräch

Bis später!	*See you later!*
Bis bald!	*See you soon!*
Bis heute Abend!	*See you this afternoon/evening!*
Bis morgen!	
Bis morgen früh!	*See you tomorrow!*
Bis Montag!	*See you Monday!*
Bis Dienstag!	*See you Tuesday!*
Bis nächste Woche!	*See you next week!*
Schönes Wochenende!	*Have a good weekend!*
Gute Ferien!	*Have a good holiday!*
Gute Reise!	*Have a good journey!*
Auf Wiedersehen!	*Goodbye!*
Tschüss!	*Cheerio!*
Tschau!	*Hi/Bye!*
Schlaf gut!	*Sleep well*

Copyright Carole Nicoll 2005

Das Alphabet

3

K.1.42 1.19 Lied

a	b	c	d	e	f	g
ah	bay	tsay	day	ay	eff	gay

h	i	j	k	l	m	n	o	p
ha	ee	yot	car	ell	emm	enn	oh	pay

q	r	s	t	u	v	w
coo	air	ess	tay	oo	fow	vay

x	y	z
ix	ypsilon	zet

Copyright Carole Nicoll 2005

Das Alphabet

Gespräch

Wie heißt du?
Ich heiße Dieter.
Wie buchstabiert man das?
Das ist D. I. E. T. E. R.

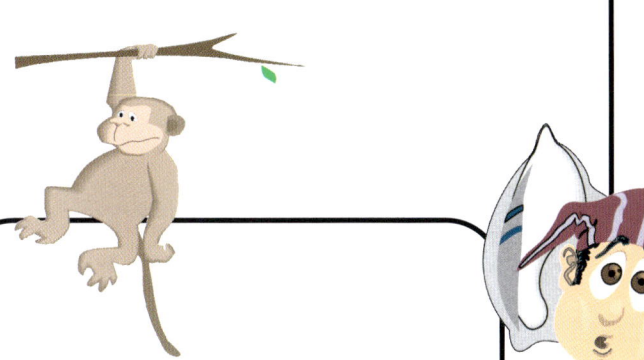

Reim ABCDE

A B C D E.
Der Kopf tut mir so weh!
F G H I K.
Der Doktor ist schon da.
L M N O.
Jetzt bin ich froh!
P Q R S T.
Es ist wieder gut! Juchhe!
U V W X.
Jetzt fehlt mir nichts!
Doch 'J' fehlt!
Y Z.
Jetzt geh' ich ins Bett!

Rap ... Die Vokale A E I O U

A E I O U Y
A E I O U Y
A E I O
A E I O
A E I O U Y

Ah ay ee oh oo oopsilon.

Volkslied ...ABC

A B C! Die Katze lief im Schnee!
Und als heraus sie wieder kam,
Da hat sie weiße Stiefel an!
O jemine! O jemine!
Die Katze lief im Schnee!

Im Klassenzimmer 5

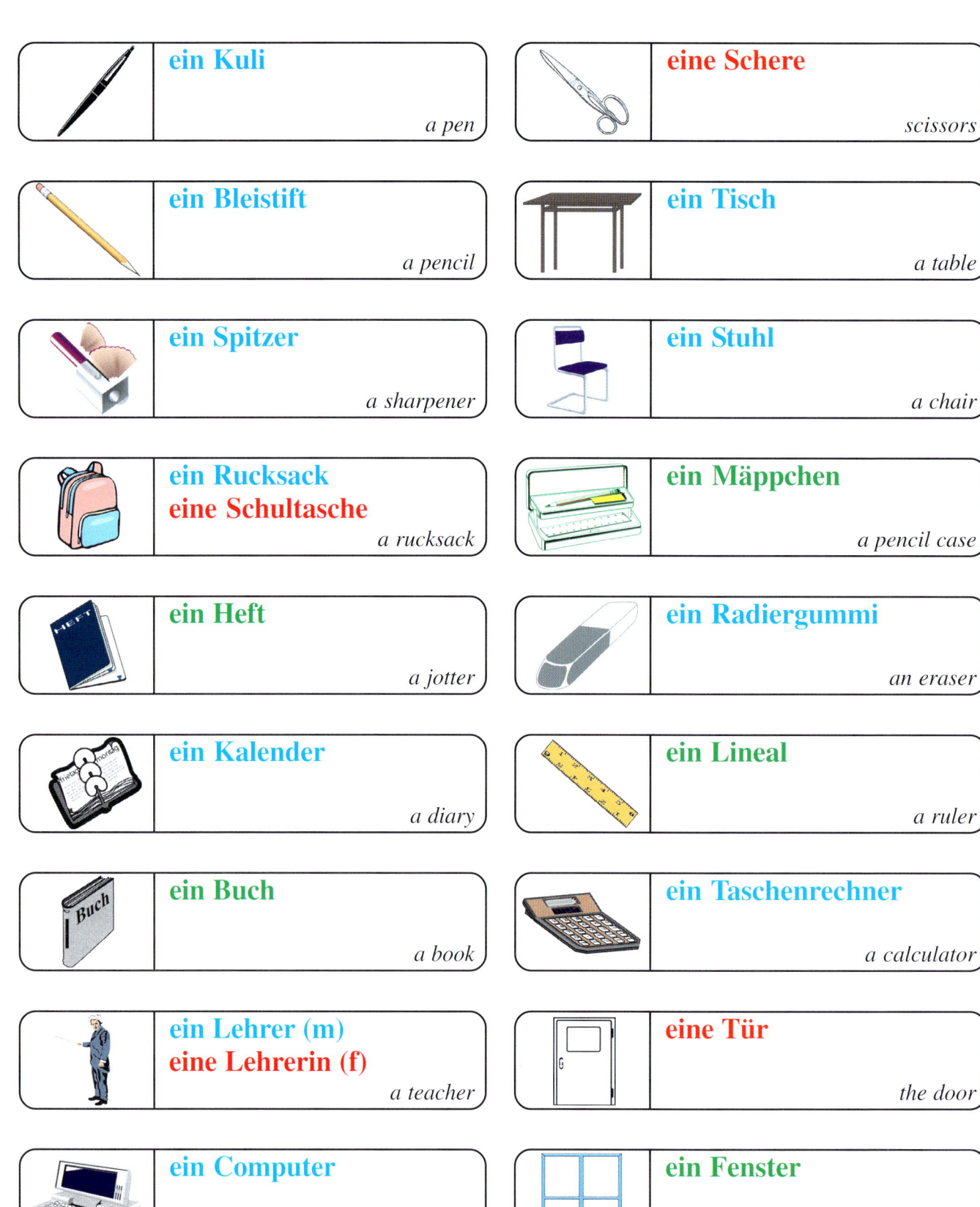

ein Kuli — *a pen*	**eine Schere** — *scissors*
ein Bleistift — *a pencil*	**ein Tisch** — *a table*
ein Spitzer — *a sharpener*	**ein Stuhl** — *a chair*
ein Rucksack / eine Schultasche — *a rucksack*	**ein Mäppchen** — *a pencil case*
ein Heft — *a jotter*	**ein Radiergummi** — *an eraser*
ein Kalender — *a diary*	**ein Lineal** — *a ruler*
ein Buch — *a book*	**ein Taschenrechner** — *a calculator*
ein Lehrer (m) / eine Lehrerin (f) — *a teacher*	**eine Tür** — *the door*
ein Computer — *a computer*	**ein Fenster** — *a window*
eine Tafel — *a white board*	**ein Papierkorb** — *a rubbish bin*

Copyright Carole Nicoll 2005

Im Klassenzimmer 6

Lied

Ein Kuli ist in meinem Mäppchen,
Ein Bleistift und Lineal.
Und ich habe auch eine Schere
Einen Spitzer, ein Radiergummi!

Was hab' ich? Wo?
Was hab' ich Wo?
Was hab' ich in meinem Mäppchen hier? (x 2)

Ein Heft habe ich in dem Rucksack
Und Hausaufgaben hab' ich auch.
Ein Buch, einen kleinen Taschenrechner,
Einen Prittstift und Tesafilm auch!

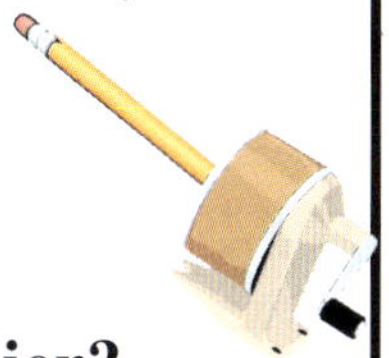

Was hab' ich? Wo?
Was hab' ich? Wo?
Was hab' ich in meinem Rucksack hier?

Im Klassenzimmer gibt's zwei Computer,
Ein Fenster und auch eine Tür.
Stühle, Tische und eine Tafel,
Einen Lehrer und Papierkorb auch!

Was hab' ich? Wo?
Was hab' ich? Wo?
Was hab' ich im Klassenzimmer!

Lied ...Von den blauen Bergen

Von den blauen Bergen kommen wir,

Unser Lehrer ist genauso dumm wie wir,

Mit dem Finger in der Nase,

Sieht er aus wie 'n Osterhase!

Von den blauen Bergen kommen wir!

Gespräch

Was hast du in deinem Rucksack?

In meinem Rucksack habe ich ein Buch, ein Heft, einen Kalender und einen Tachenrechner.

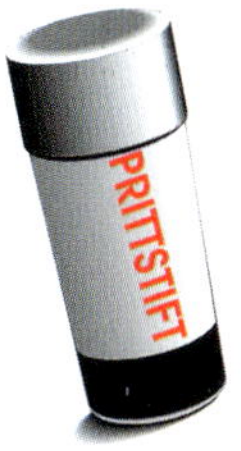

Was gibt's in dem Klassenzimmer?

In dem Klassenzimmer gibt's Stühle, Tische, einen Lehrer und einen Papierkorb!

Gespräch

Was ist das?

Das ist ein Computer!

Was hast du in deinem Mäppchen?

In meinem Mäppchen gibt's einen Kuli, einen Spitzer, einen Radiergummi und eine Schere!

Copyright Carole Nicoll 2005

Tiere 7

eine Katze — *a cat*		**ein Kaninchen** — *a rabbit*	
ein Hund — *a dog*		**eine Schlange** — *a snake*	
ein Hamster — *a hamster*		**ein Vogel** — *a bird*	
ein Pony / Pferd — *a pony / horse*		**ein Kätzchen** — *a kitten*	
ein Meerschweinchen — *a guinea pig*		**ein Hündchen** — *a puppy*	
ein Papagei — *a parrot*		**ein Fretchen** — *a ferret*	
ein Fisch — *a fish*		**eine Schildkröte** — *a tortoise*	
eine Eidechse — *a lizard*		**eine Maus** — *a mouse*	
eine Ratte — *a rat*		**ein Wellensittich** — *a budgie*	
eine Gespenstheuschrecke — *a stick insect*		**eine Wüstenspringmaus** — *a gerbil*	

Copyright Carole Nicoll 2005

Tiere

Gespräch

Hast du ein Haustier?

Ja, ich habe einen Hund.

Ach ja, wie heißt er?

Er heißt Max.

Welche Farbe hat er?

Er ist weiß.

Wie alt ist er?

Er ist neun!

Hast du ein Haustier?

Nein, ich habe keine Haustiere!

Ach, wie schade!

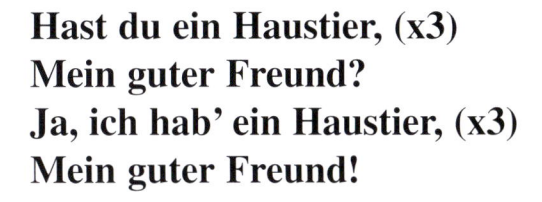

Rap

Hast du ein Haustier, (x3)
Mein guter Freund?
Ja, ich hab' ein Haustier, (x3)
Mein guter Freund!

Ich habe eine Katze.
Ich habe eine Schlange.
Ich habe eine Ratte.
Und auch eine Maus!

Ich habe einen Goldfisch.
Ich habe einen Hamster.
Ich habe einen Vogel.
Und auch einen Hund!

Hast du ein Haustier, (x3)
Mein guter Freund?
Nein, ich habe keine! (x3)
Wie schade, mein Freund!

Farben

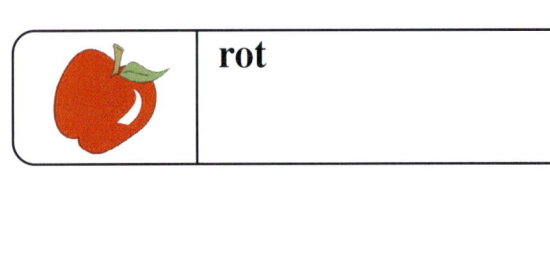

rot — *red*	**grün** — *green*
gelb — *yellow*	**blau** — *blue*
schwarz — *black*	**rosa** — *pink*
weiß — *white*	**braun** — *brown*
lila — *purple*	**grau** — *grey*
orange — *orange*	**silber** — *silver*
gold — *gold*	**hellblau** — *light blue*

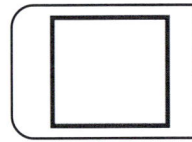

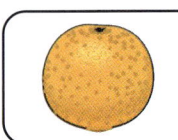

dunkelblau *navy blue*   **dunkelgrün** *dark green*   **kariert** *tartan*   **rostfarben** *rust*   **bunt** *multi-coloured*

Copyright Carole Nicoll 2005

Farben

Reim

An der Ampel
Bei rot musst du stehen.
Bei grün darfst du gehen!
Gute Reise!

Gespräch

Was ist deine Lieblingsfarbe?
Meine Lieblingsfarbe ist schwarz.
Was sind deine Lieblingsfarben?
Meine Lieblingsfarben sind schwarz und weiß!

Lied ...Was ist gelb?

Was ist gelb? Was ist gelb?
Weißt du das? Weißt du das?
Bananen und Zitronen.
Bananen und Zitronen.
Sonnenschein!
Sonnenschein!

Was ist grün? Was ist grün?
Weißt du das? Weißt du das?
Gras und Äpfel.
Gras und Äpfel.
Trauben auch!
Trauben auch!

Was ist rot? Was ist rot?
Weißt du das? Weißt du das?
Kirschen und Tomaten!
Kirschen und Tomaten!
Erdbeeren auch!
Erdbeeren auch!

Lied ...Lieblingsfarbe

Was ist deine Lieblingsfarbe, Hans?
Schwarz, lila, braun?
Rot, gelb, weiß, blau?
Was ist deine Lieblingsfarbe, Hans?
Lila, orange oder hellblau?

Meine Lieblingsfarbe ist doch rot,
Meine Lieblingsfarbe ist doch rosa,
Meine Lieblingsfarbe ist doch gelb,
Meine Lieblingsfarbe ist doch blau!

Copyright Carole Nicoll 2005

Farben

Reim

Das Gras ist grün.
Die See ist blau.
Der Sand ist gelb.
Die Maus ist grau.
Der Bär ist braun.
Die Rose rot.
Die Kohle schwarz,
Und weiß das Brot!

Volkslied...Grün Grün Grün

Grün, grün, grün sind alle meine Kleider.
Grün, grün, grün ist alles was ich hab'!

Darum lieb' ich alles, was so grün ist,
Weil mein Schatz ein Jäger, Jäger ist! (x2)

Blau, blau, blau, sind alle meine Kleider…..
Weil mein Schatz ein Matrose ist!

Weiß, weiß, weiß sind alle meine Kleider….
Weil mein Schatz ein Bäcker, Bäcker ist!

Schwarz, schwarz, schwarz sind alle meine Kleider….
Weil mein Schatz ein Schornsteinfeger ist!

Rot, rot, rot, sind alle meine Kleider….
Weil mein Schatz ein Feuerwehrmann ist!

Bunt, bunt, bunt sind alle meine Kleider….
Weil mein Schatz ein Maler, Maler ist!

Gespräch

Welche Farbe ist das?
Das ist rosa! Das ist orange!
Was sind die Farben der deutschen Fahne?
Schwarz, rot, gold…. Natürlich!

Lied...Welche Farbe ist das?

Welche Farbe, welche Farbe,
welche Farbe ist das? (x4)

Rot, gelb, grün und blau (x4)

Schwarz, weiß, rosa, braun (x4)

Orange, lila, grau (x4)

Silber, gold, hellblau (x4)

Tage

Montag — *Monday*

Dienstag — *Tuesday*

Mittwoch — *Wednesday*

Donnerstag — *Thursday*

Freitag — *Friday*

Samstag — *Saturday*

Sonntag — *Sunday*

das Wochenende — *the weekend*

- **der Tag** *the day*
- **die Woche** *the week*
- **gestern** *yesterday*
- **heute** *today*
- **morgen** *tomorrow*

Gespräch

Welchen Tag haben wir heute?
Heute ist Montag.
Und gestern?
Gestern war Sonntag.
Und morgen?
Morgen ist doch Dienstag. (Mensch!)

Lied

...Die Tage

Montag, Dienstag, Mittwoch
Donnerstag, Freitag, Samstag.
Sag mal, was fehlt uns
immer noch? (x2)
Was? Was fehlt uns noch?
Was fehlt uns noch?
Ach, ja! Sonntag! (x2)

Copyright Carole Nicoll 2005

Monate

Januar		Juli
	January	

January

Februar
February

März
March

April
April

Mai
May

Juni
June

Juli
July

August
August

September
September

Oktober
October

November
November

Dezember
December

Gespräch

Was ist dein Lieblingsmonat?

Mein Lieblingsmonat ist Juli.

Warum?

Das Wetter ist schön und ich habe Geburtstag.

Lied

...Januar, Februar

Januar, Februar, März, April, Mai.
Juni, Juli, August! (x 2)
September, Oktober.
November, Dezember.
Juni, Juli, August! (x 2)
Januar, Februar, März, April, Mai.
Juni, Juli, August! (x 2)

Mein Geburtstag

Gespräch

Wann hast du Geburtstag?

Ich habe am neunzehnten August Geburtstag!

Gespräch

Alles Gute zum Geburtstag!
Ja, viel Glück!
Was hast du zum Geburtstag bekommen?
Ich habe ein Handy bekommen!
Oh! Toll!

Lied
...Zum Geburtstag viel Glück!

Zum Geburtstag, viel Glück! (x 2)
Zum Geburtstag, lieber Dietrich!
Zum Geburtstag, viel Glück!

Zum Geburtstag, viel Glück! (x 2)
Zum Geburtstag, liebe Anna!
Zum Geburtstag, viel Glück!

Lied
...Wer im Januar

Wer im Januar geboren ist,
Steh auf! Steh auf! Steh auf!
Wer im Februar geboren ist,
Steh auf! Steh auf! Steh auf!
Wer im März…..
Wer im April….
Wer im Mai……
Wer im Juni……
Wer im Juli……
Wer im August…
Wer im September…
Wer im Oktober…
Wer im November…
Wer im Dezember geboren ist,
Steh auf! Steh auf! Steh auf!

Lied
...Ersten, zweiten, dritten.

Ersten, zweiten, dritten, vierten.
Fünften, sechsten, siebten, achten.
Neunten, zehnten, elften, zwölften.
Wann hast du Geburtstag?
Dreizehnten, vierzehnten?
Sechzehnten, siebzehnten?
Neunzehnten, zwanzigsten?
Wann hast du Geburtstag?
Einundzwanzigsten Juni?
Oder dreißigsten Juni?
Einunddreißigsten Juli?
Wann hast du Geburtstag?

Copyright Carole Nicoll 2005

Jahreszeiten

im Herbst — *in autumn*

im Winter — *in winter*

im Frühling — *in spring*

im Sommer — *in summer*

Gespräch

Der Herbst, der Winter,
Der Frühling, der Sommer.
In welcher Jahreszeit hast du Geburtstag?
Ich habe im Frühling Geburtstag.
Wie ist das Wetter im Frühling?
Es ist schön, aber es regnet.
Wann ist deine Lieblingsjahreszeit?
Meine Lieblingsjahreszeit ist der Herbst.
Warum?
Den Wind und die Wolken habe ich gern!
Wirklich?

Volkslied ...Summ summ summ!

Summ, summ, summ,
Bienchen summ herum!
Such' in Blumen,
Such' in Blümchen,
Dir ein Tröpfchen,
Dir ein Krümchen!
Summ, summ, summ,
Bienchen summ herum!

Volkslied ...Ja ja ja! Der Sommertag ist da!

Ja! Ja! Ja! Der Sommertag ist da!
Wir wollen in den Garten
Wir wollen nicht mehr warten!
Ja! Ja! Ja! Der Sommertag ist da!

Ja! Ja! Ja! Der Sommertag ist da!
Der Sommer hat gewonnen!
Der Winter hat verloren!
Ja! Ja! Ja! Der Sommertag ist da!

Copyright Carole Nicoll 2005

Jahreszeiten

Reim .....Gelbes Blatt, falle ab.

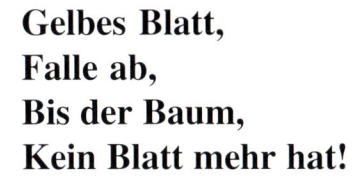

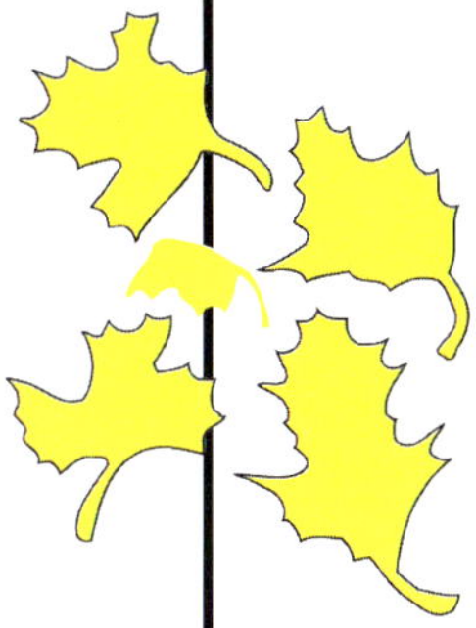

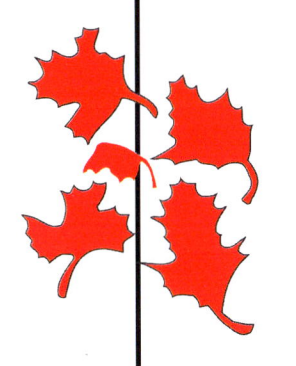

Gelbes Blatt,
Falle ab,
Bis der Baum,
Kein Blatt mehr hat!

Rotes Blatt,
Falle ab,
Bis der Baum,
Kein Blatt mehr hat!

Buntes Blatt,
Falle ab,
Bis der Baum,
Kein Blatt mehr hat!

Volkslied ...Kuckuck! Kuckuck!

Kuckuck! Kuckuck!
Ruft's aus dem Wald.
Lasset uns singen, tanzen und springen!
Frühling! Frühling!
Wird es nun bald!

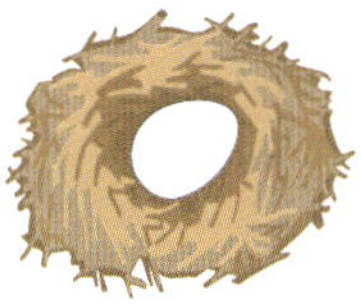

Volkslied ...Alle Vögel sind schon da!

Alle Vögel sind schon da!
Alle Vögel, alle!
Amsel, Drossel, Fink und Star,
Und die ganze Vogelschar,
Wünschen dir ein frohes Jahr,
Lauter Heil und Segen!

Reim .....Ru Ru Risch!

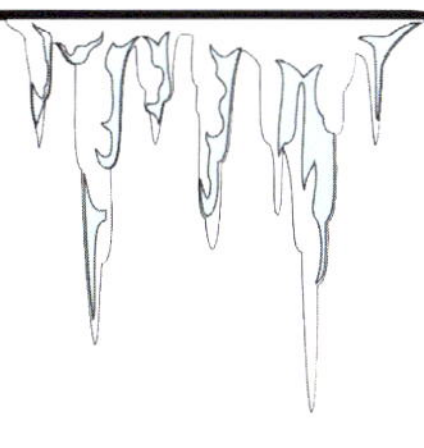

Ru ru risch,
Im Winter ist es frisch.
Im Sommer singt die Nachtigall.
Da freuen sich die Vögel all!
Ru ru risch,
Im Winter ist es frisch!

Copyright Carole Nicoll 2005

Das Wetter — 17

German	English	German	English
Es ist heiß.	It is hot	Es ist wolkig.	It is grey
Es ist sonnig	It is sunny	Es ist dunkel	It is dark
Es ist schön.	It is fine	der Himmel	the sky
Es ist kalt.	It is cold	der Bauer	the farmer
Es regnet.	It is raining	der Baum	the tree
Es schneit.	It is snowing	die Blume	the flower
Es ist windig.	It is windy	der Regenschirm	the umbrella
Es ist wolkig.	It is cloudy	der Frosch	the frog
Es ist schlecht.	It is bad weather	der Regen	the rain
Es ist neblig.	It is foggy	die komische Insel	Crazy Island!

Copyright Carole Nicoll 2005

Das Wetter 18

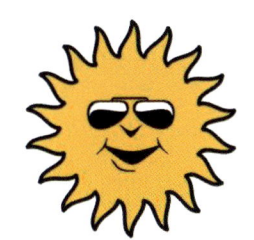

Gespräch

Wie ist das Wetter in Afrika?

In Afrika ist es heiß und sonnig, aber manchmal regnet es.

Wie ist das Wetter in Island?

In Island ist es kalt und es schneit, aber manchmal ist es heiß.

Lied
...Das Wetter

Wie ist das Wetter? Wie ist das Wetter?
Es ist heiß! Es ist heiß!
Heute scheint die Sonne! (x2)
Es ist heiß! Es ist heiß!

Wie ist das Wetter? Wie ist das Wetter?
Es ist kalt! (x2)
Es schneit, es schneit, es regnet! (x2)
Es ist kalt! (x2)

Wie ist das Wetter? Wie ist das Wetter?
Windig und kühl! (x2)
Und es ist auch wolkig! (x2)
Windig und kühl!

Wie ist das Wetter? Wie ist das Wetter?
Es ist schlecht! x 2
Und es ist sehr neblig! (x2)
Was für ein Tag! (x2)

Copyright Carole Nicoll 2005

Das Wetter

Reim

Weiß wie Kreide,
Leicht wie Flaum,
Weich wie Seide,
Feucht wie Schaum.
Der Schnee! Der Schnee!
Auf jedem Baum.

Volkslied

...Schneewalzer

Wenn im Frühling Blumen blühn,
Und die Bäume werden grün,
Wenn ein Vogel singt im Wald,
Scheint die Sommersonne bald!
Wenn das Herbstlaub langsam fällt,
Und der Winter Einzug hält,
Liegt der Schnee auf Wald und Feld.
Ach, wie schön ist doch diese Welt.

Schnee, Schnee, Schnee, Schnee-
Walzer, tanzen wir.
Du mit mir. Ich mit dir!
Schnee, Schnee, Schnee, Schnee-
Walzer, tanzen wir.
Und seit dieser Zeit da gehöre ich immer dir!

Das Wetter

Reim.....Imse Wimse Spinne

Imse Wimse Spinne.
Wie lang dein Faden ist!
Kam der Regen runter,
Und der Faden riss!
Dann kam die Sonne,
Leckt den Regen auf!
Imse Wimse Spinne,
Klettert wieder auf!

Gespräch

Wie ist das Wetter heute?
Heute ist es schlecht!
Wie ist das Wetter im Herbst?
Im Herbst ist es windig und schlecht!
Wie ist das Wetter im Winter?
Im Winter ist es kalt und es schneit!
Wie ist das Wetter im Frühling?
Im Frühling regnet es.
Wie ist das Wetter im Sommer?
Im Sommer ist es heiß und sonnig.
Wie ist das Wetter in Schottland?
In Schottland!
Ach, es ist oft neblig
und immer wolkig!

Volkslied ...Es regnet

Es regnet! Es regnet!
Es regnet seinen Lauf,
Und wenn's genug geregnet hat,
Dann hört es wieder auf!

Reim

Wenn die Sonne scheint,
Ist der Himmel klar.
Wenn der Regen kommt,
Sind die Wolken da!

Reim

Schneeflöckchen!
Weißröckchen!
Komm zu uns ins Tal!
Dann bauen wir den
Schneemann,
Und werfen wir den Ball!

Copyright Carole Nicoll 2005

Wie siehst du aus? 21

Ich habe **schwarze** Haare. *I have black hair.*	Ich habe **schwarze** Augen. *I have black eyes.*
Ich habe **blonde** Haare. *I have blond hair.*	Ich habe **braune** Augen. *I have brown eyes.*
Ich habe **rote** Haare. *I have red hair.*	Ich habe **graue** Augen. *I have grey eyes.*
Ich habe **braune** Haare. *I have brown hair.*	Ich bin **groß**. *I am big.*
Ich habe **lange** Haare. *I have long hair.*	Ich bin **klein**. *I am small.*
Ich habe **kurze** Haare. *I have short hair.*	Ich trage eine **Brille**. *I wear glasses.*
Ich habe **glatte** Haare. *I have straight hair.*	Ich bin **nett**. *I am nice.*
Ich habe **lockige** Haare. *I have curly hair.*	Ich bin **frech**. *I am naughty.*
Ich habe **blaue** Augen. *I have blue eyes.*	Ich trage **Ohrringe**. *I wear earrings.*
Ich habe **grüne** Augen. *I have green eyes.*	Ich trage eine **Armbanduhr**. *I wear a watch.*

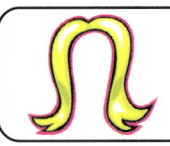

Copyright Carole Nicoll 2005

Wie siehst du aus ? | 22

Gespräch

Wie siehst du aus?
Ich habe kurze, glatte, shwarze Haare.
Und du? Wie siehst du aus?

Ich habe blaue Augen.
Und du da drüben?
Ich bin ganz groß und nett.
Und du? ....
Ich trage eine Brille.

Lied...Wie siehst du aus?

Wie siehst du aus? (x5)
Hab' schwarze Haare.
Hab' blonde Haare.
Hab' rote Haare.
Hab' braune Haare.

Wie siehst du aus? (x5)
Hab' lange Haare.
Hab' kurze Haare.
Hab' glatte Haare.
Hab' lockige Haare.

Wie siehst du aus? (x5)
Hab' blaue Augen.
Hab' grüne Augen.
Hab' graue Augen.
Hab' braune Augen.

Wie siehst du aus? (x5)
Ich bin ganz groß.
Ich bin sehr klein.
Ich trag' eine Brille.
Ich bin aber nett!

Volkslied...Spannenlanger Hansel

Spannenlanger Hansel,
nudeldicke Dirn.
Geh'n wir in den Garten.
Schütteln wir die Birn!
Schüttelst du die großen,

Schüttel ich die klein,
Wenn das Säcklein voll ist,
Geh'n wir wieder heim!

Lauf doch nicht so närrisch,
spannenlanger Hans.
Ich verlier die Birnen und die Schuh noch ganz!
Trägst ja nur die kleinen, nudeldicke Dirn,
Und ich schlepp den schweren Sack,
Mit den großen Birn!

Zungenbrecher

Unter dichten Fichtenwurzeln hören wir die Wichtel furzen.

Copyright Carole Nicoll 2005

Die Familie

mein Vater	my father
meine Mutter	my mother
mein Bruder	my brother
eine Schwester	my sister
mein Großvater	my grandfather
meine Großmutter	my grandmother
mein Onkel	my uncle
meine Tante	my aunt
mein Vetter	my cousin (boy)
meine Cousine	my cousin (girl)
mein Stiefbruder	my step-brother
meine Stiefschwester	my step-sister
mein Stiefvater	my step-father
meine Stiefmutter	my step-mother
mein Stiefsohn	my step-son
meine Stieftochter	my step-daughter
mein Neffe	my nephew
meine Nichte	my niece
ein Baby	a baby
ein Teenager	a teenager

Copyright Carole Nicoll 2005

Die Familie

Gespräch

Hast du Geschwister?
Ja, ich habe einen Bruder und eine Schwester.
Wie heißt dein Bruder?
Er heißt Peter.

Wie heißt deine Schwester?
Sie heißt Eva.
Wie alt ist sie?
Sie ist zwölf Jahre alt.

Lied...Bruder, Vater, Großvater

Bruder, Vater, Großvater.
Schwester, Mutter, Großmutter.
Tante, Onkel, Kusine.
Vetter und auch Stiefbruder.

Hast du Geschwister, Hans?
Ja, ich habe einen Bruder.
Hast du Geschwister, Jens?
Ja, ich habe eine Schwester,
Ein Hündchen,
Ein Kätzchen,
Kaninchen und
Meerschweinchen.
Hast du Geschwister, Kind?
Nein, ich bin Einzelkind!

Reim und Volkslied ...Es war eine Mutter

Es war eine Mutter,
Die hatte vier Kinder.
Den Frühling, den Sommer,
Den Herbst und den Winter.

Der Frühling bringt Blumen.
Der Sommer den Klee.
Der Herbst, der bringt Trauben.
Der Winter den Schnee!

Copyright Carole Nicoll 2005

Das Café

25

ein Hotdog	a hotdog
ein Butterbrot mit Schinken	a ham baguette
Käsetoast	cheese on toast
ein Hamburger	a hamburger
Weißwein	some white wine
eine Cola — 'besser geht's mit Coca Cola!'	a coca cola — "It's the real thing"
ein Kaffee	a coffee
ein Tee	a tea
ein Kellner	a waiter
eine Wurst	a sausage
Milch	some milk
Orangensaft	orange juice
ein Kuchen	a cake
Wasser	water
die Rechnung	the bill
Pommes Frites	some chips
ein Berliner	a doughnut
eine Limo	a lemonade
ein Eis	an ice-cream
ein Bier	a beer

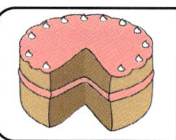

Copyright Carole Nicoll 2005

Das Café

Gespräch

Herr Ober!
Guten Abend!
Kann ich Ihnen helfen?
Ja, bitte!
Was möchten Sie?
Ich möchte einen Kaffee, bitte. 
Und Sie? Was möchten Sie?
Ich hätte gern eine Cola bitte.
So, bitte schön.
Vielen Dank.
Guten Appetit!
Herr Ober! Die Rechnung, bitte!
.....Danke.
Meine Güte, ist das teuer!

Lied ...Wir haben Hunger

Wir haben Hunger, Hunger, Hunger, haben Durst! (x 2)
Wir haben Hunger, Hunger, Hunger,
bring das Wasser, bring die Wurst!
Wir haben Hunger, Hunger, Hunger, haben Durst!

Wir haben Hunger, Hunger, Hunger, haben Durst! (x 2)
Wir haben Hunger, Hunger, Hunger,
bring den Saft und bring die Wurst!
Wir haben Hunger, Hunger, Hunger,
haben Durst! (x 2)

Wir haben Hunger, Hunger, Hunger, haben Durst! (x 2)
Wir haben Hunger, Hunger, Hunger,
bring das Bier und bring die Wurst!
Wir haben Hunger, Hunger, Hunger,
haben Durst!

Wir haben Hunger, Hunger, Hunger, haben Durst! (x 2)
Wir haben Hunger, Hunger, Hunger,
bring den Wein und bring die Wurst!
Wir haben Hunger, Hunger, Hunger,
haben Durst!

Lied ...Das Café

Guten Abend!
Was möchten
Sie, mein Herr?
(x 2)

Ich möchte einen Tee,
Und einen Kaffee.

Einen Hamburger,
Einen Berliner.

Bier für meine Frau,
Eine Limo auch,

Butterbrot mit
Schinken für mich!
(x2)

Bitte sehr!

Reim...Kein Wein...

'Kein Wein', sagt das Schwein!
'Wo werden wir tanzen?'
sagen die Wanzen

'Im Haus' sagt die Maus
'Auf dem Tisch'
sagt der Fisch!

Copyright Carole Nicoll 2005

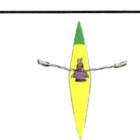

Sportarten 27

Fußball	Kanufahren
football	*canoeing*

Squash	Golf
squash	*golf*

Snowboarden	Laufen
snowboarding	*running*

Skateboarden	Schwimmen
skateboarding	*swimming*

Radfahren	Angeln
cycling	*fishing*

Tennis	Gymnastik
tennis	*gymnastics*

Rugby	Boxen
rugby	*boxing*

Schlittschuhlaufen	Leichtathletik
ice skating	*athletics*

Hockey	Judo
hockey	*judo*

Ringen	Segeln
wrestling	*sailing*

Copyright Carole Nicoll 2005

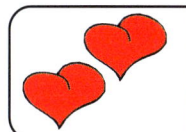

Sportarten

28

Ich liebe — *I adore*	**Ich hasse** — *I hate*
Ich habe...gern — *I like*	**Ich ziehe...vor** — *I prefer*
Ich habe...nicht gern — *I don't like*	**Reiten** — *horse-riding*

Rap ...Sportarten

Welchen Sport hast du am liebsten?
Tennis, Rugby, Hockey, Schwimmen?
Snowboard, Rad, Kanu fahren?
Golf hab' ich nicht gern!

Welchen Sport hast du am liebsten?
Segeln, Laufen, Boxen, Reiten?
Skateboard oder Schlittschuhlaufen?
Ringen hab' ich gern!

Ich ziehe Squash und Judo vor,
Ich liebe Angeln und Fußball!
Ich habe Leichtathletik gern
Ich hasse Gymnastik!

Gespräch 1

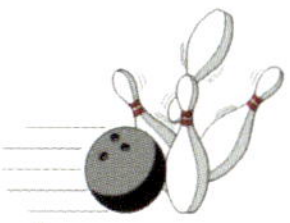

Was ist dein Lieblingssport?
Fußball!
Welche Sportarten hast du nicht gern?
Kegeln habe ich nicht gern!
Welche Sportarten hasst du?
Ich hasse Golf!

Gespräch 2

Was ist dein Lieblingssport?
Radfahren! Und deiner?
Ich ziehe Schlittschuhlaufen vor!
Warum?
Es ist lustig und schwierig!

Vokabeln

leicht	*easy*	**lustig**	*fun, funny*	**super**	*brilliant*	**fantastisch**	*great*
schwierig	*difficult*	**langweilig**	*boring*	**schrecklich**	*awful*	**aufregend**	*exciting*

Die Zeit

Es ist ein Uhr. *It is one o'clock.*

Es ist acht Uhr. *It is eight o'clock.*

Es ist vier Uhr. *It is four o'clock.*

Es ist Mittag. *It is midday.*

Es ist Mitternacht. *It is midnight.*

Guten Morgen! *Good morning!*

Guten Tag, Guten Abend! *Good afternoon, Good evening!*

Es ist halb neun. *It is half past eight.*

Es ist Viertel nach acht. *It is quarter past eight.*

Es ist fünf nach halb acht. *It is twenty-five to eight.*

Es ist Viertel vor acht. *It is quarter to eight.*

Es ist zehn nach acht. *It is ten past eight.*

Es ist zwanzig nach acht. *It is twenty past eight.*

Gute Nacht! *Good night!*

Gespräch ...Mein Tagesablauf

3.24

Wann verlässt du das Haus?
Ich verlasse das Haus um sieben Uhr.
Wann isst du Mittagessen?
Ich esse um ein Uhr.
Wann kommst du wieder nach Hause?
Ich komme um vier Uhr nach Hause.
Wann isst du Abendessen?
Ich esse um sieben Uhr.
Wann gehst du ins Bett?
Ich gehe um zehn Uhr ins Bett

Die Zeit

Volkslied
...Große Uhren

Große Uhren gehen
ticke tacke ticke tacke.
Kleine Uhren gehen
ticketacke ticketacke.
Und die ganz, ganz kleinen Uhren gehen
ticketacke ticketacke ticketacke tick!

Gespräch

Wie spät ist es, bitte?
Es ist acht Uhr.

Lied
..... die Zeit

Hallo, wie spät ist es? (x2)
Es ist acht Uhr. (x2)
Hallo, wie spät ist es?

Hallo, wie spät ist es? (x2)
Es ist Mittag. (x2)
Hallo, wie spät ist es?

N'Abend, wie spät ist es? (x2)
Neunzehn Uhr. (x2)
N'Abend, wie spät ist es?

Hallo, wie spät ist es? (x2)
Mitternacht. (x 2)
Hallo, wie spät ist es?

Halb neun, fünf nach acht,
Viertel vor acht, viertel nach acht,
Zehn nach acht und zehn nach neun.
Hallo, wie spät ist es?

Reim

Morgens früh um sechs,
Kommt die kleine Hex!
Morgens früh um sieben,
Schält sie gelbe Rüb'n!
Morgens früh um acht,
Wird Kaffee gemacht!
Morgens früh um neun,
Geht sie in die Scheun!
Morgens früh um zehn,
Holt sie Holz und Spän!
Feuert an um elf,
Kocht dann bis um zwölf,
Fröschebein und Krebs und Fisch!
Hurtig, Kinder, kommt zu Tisch!

Copyright Carole Nicoll 2005

In meinem Schlafzimmer — 31

ein Bett — a bed	ein Vorhang — a curtain
ein Sessel — an armchair	ein Kleiderschrank — a wardrobe
ein Teppich — a rug	ein Fernseher — a television
ein Federbett — a duvet	ein großes Plüschtier — a big, fat, soft toy
ein Waschbecken — a wash basin	ein Bücherregal / ein Regal — a bookshelf
ein Schreibtisch — a desk	eine Dusche — a shower
ein Kissen — a pillow	ein Stuhl — a chair
ein Eisschrank — a fridge	eine Lampe — a lamp
eine Schublade — a drawer	eine Kommode — a chest of drawers
ein Sofa — a sofa	eine Stereoanlage — a hi fi

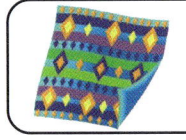

Copyright Carole Nicoll 2005

In meinem Schlafzimmer 32

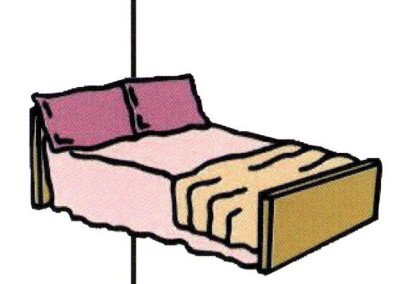

Gespräch

Wie ist dein Zimmer?

Es ist ziemlich klein.

Was hast du in deinem Zimmer?

In meinem Zimmer, habe ich ein Regal, ein großes Bett und einen Fernseher.

Einen Fernseher! Du hast aber Glück!

Schlaflied...Schlaf Kindchen schlaf!

Schlaf, Kindchen, schlaf!
Dein Vater hüt't die Schaf.
Die Mutter schüttelt's Bäumelein,
Da fällt herab ein Träumelein!
Schlaf, Kindchen, schlaf!

Maikäfer flieg!

Maikäfer flieg!
Dein Vater ist im Krieg.
Die Mutter ist in Pommerland,
Pommerland ist abgebrannt!
Maikäfer flieg!

Copyright Carole Nicoll 2005

Verkehrsmittel 33

das Segelboot *the boat* mit dem Segelboot *by boat*	**das Dreirad** *the tricycle* mit dem Dreirad *by tricycle*
das Fahrrad *the bicycle* mit dem Fahrrad *by bicycle*	**der Dampfer** *the liner* mit dem Dampfer *by liner*
der Bus *the bus* mit dem Bus *by bus*	**die U-Bahn** *the rocket* mit der U-Bahn *on the tube*
der Zug *the train* mit dem Zug *by train*	**der Heißluftballon** *the hot air balloon* mit dem Heißluftballon *by hot air balloon*
das Pony *the pony* mit dem Pony *by pony*	**das Auto/der Wagen** *the car* mit dem Auto/mit dem Wagen *by car*
das Flugzeug *the airplane* mit dem Flugzeug *by air*	**das Mofa** *the moped* mit dem Mofa *by moped*
der Fuß *the feet* zu Fuß *by foot*	**die Rakete** *the rocket* mit einer Rakete *by rocket*
die Rollschuhe *the rollerskates* auf Rollschuhen *on rollerskates*	**das Motorrad** *the motorcycle* mit dem Motorrad *by motorcycle*
der Reisebus *the coach* mit dem Reisebus *by coach*	**das Raumschiff** *the spaceship* mit dem Raumschiff *by spaceship*
der Lastwagen *the lorry* mit dem Lastwagen *by lorry*	**die fliegende Untertasse** *the flying saucer* mit einer fliegenden Untertasse *by flying saucer*

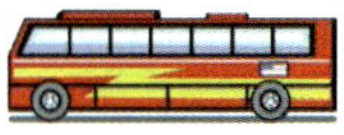

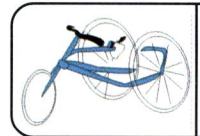

Copyright Carole Nicoll 2005

Verkehrsmittel

Gespräch

Wie kommst du zur Schule?
Ich komme mit dem Auto.
Wie kommst du zur Schule?
Ich fahre mit dem Bus, aber manchmal gehe ich zu Fuß.
Ich fahre auch mit dem Zug von Zeit zu Zeit!
Kommst du mit einer fliegenden Untertasse?
Mit einer fliegenden Untertasse? Nie!

Lied
...Die Reifen am Bus

Die Reifen am Bus machen
plitsch, platsch, plitsch. (x3)
Die Reifen am Bus machen
plitsch, platsch, plitsch.
Den lieben langen Tag!

Der Motor am Bus macht
brumm, brumm, brumm. (x3)
Der Motor am Bus macht
brumm, brumm, brumm.
Den lieben langen Tag!

Copyright Carole Nicoll 2005

Verkehrsmittel 35

Lied
...Meine Oma fährt Motorrad

Meine Oma fährt im Hühnerstall Motorrad!
Motorrad! Motorrad!
Meine Oma fährt im Hühnerstall Motorrad!
Meine Oma ist 'ne ganz moderne Frau!

Meine Oma hat im hohlen Zahn ein Radio!

Meine Oma hat 'nen Nachttopf mit Beleuchtung!

Meine Oma hat 'ne Brille mit Gardine!

Volkslied
...Mein Bonnie

Mein Bonnie ist weit von der Heimat.
Mein Bonnie ist weit auf dem Meer!
Ihr Winde und wogenden Wasser,
O bringt ihn mir doch wieder her!
Bringt ihn, bringt ihn,
O bringt ihn mir doch wieder her! Wieder her!
Bringt ihn, bringt ihn,
O bringt ihn mir doch wieder her!

Verkehrsmittel 36

Volkslied

...Sag mir, was machen die Matrosen?

Sag mir! Was machen die Matrosen,
Norweger, Deutsche und Franzosen,
Wenn auf dem Meer die Wellen tosen,
Morgens in der Frühe?
Ho-he, und hoch die Segel! (x3)
Morgens in der Frühe!

Würden so gern den Mädchen winken,
Rum oder Schnapps oder Whisky trinken,
Lieber als im Meer versinken,
Morgens in der Frühe!
Ho-he, und hoch die Gläser! (x3)
Morgens in der Frühe!

Der Körper

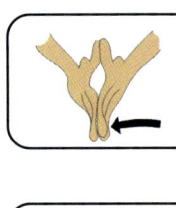

der Finger	finger	die Nase	nose
das Kinn	chin	der Rücken	back
das Knie	knee	der Ellenbogen	elbow
Zehen	toes	das Herz	heart
der Hals	neck	die Hand	hand
Augen	eyes	der Mund	mouth
der Arm	arm	das Bein	legs
Haare	hair	der Kopf	head
der Fuß	foot	das Ohr	ear
die Stirn	forehead	Schultern	shoulders

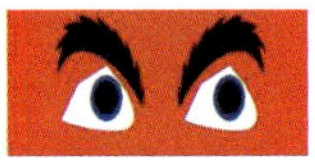

Der Körper 38

Gespräch

Was ist das?
Das ist mein Kopf!
Was ist das?
Das ist meine Nase!
Was ist das?
Das ist mein Ohr!

Lied... Kopf, Schultern, Knie und Zehen

Kopf, Schultern, Knie und Zehen, Knie und Zehen! (x2)
Augen, Ohren, Nase, Mund und Kinn, Kopf, Schultern, Knie und Zehen
Knie und Zehen!

Lied ...Schwuppi Wuppi (The Hokey Cokey)

Wir tun die rechte Hand rein,
Die rechte Hand raus,
Hinein, hinaus,
Und schütteln wir sie aus.
Wir machen Schwuppi Wuppi,
Und wir dreh'n uns um.
So wird das gemacht!

Oh! Schwuppi, Wuppi, Wuppi! (x 3)
So wird das gemacht!

Wir tun den linken Fuß rein,
Den linken Fuß raus,
Hinein, hinaus,
Und schütteln wir ihn aus.
Wir machen Schwuppi Wuppi,
Und wir dreh'n uns um.
So wird das gemacht!

Wir tun das rechte Ohr rein,
Das rechte Ohr raus,
Hinein, hinaus,
Und schütteln wir es aus.
Wir machen Schwuppi Wuppi,
Und wir dreh'n uns um.
So wird das gemacht!

Wir tun den Popo rein,
Den Popo raus,
Hinein, hinaus,
Und schütteln wir ihn aus.
Wir machen Schwuppi Wuppi,
Und wir dreh'n uns um.
So wird das gemacht!

Copyright Carole Nicoll 2005

Der Körper

Lied
...Hans sagt

Hans sagt: 'Zeig mir den Kopf
Und die Nase auch!'
Hans sagt: 'Zeig mir den Mund
Und die Ohren auch!'
Hans sagt: 'Zeig mir die Hand
Und die Augen auch!'
Hans sagt: 'Zeig mir die Stirn sofort
Und die Haare auch!'

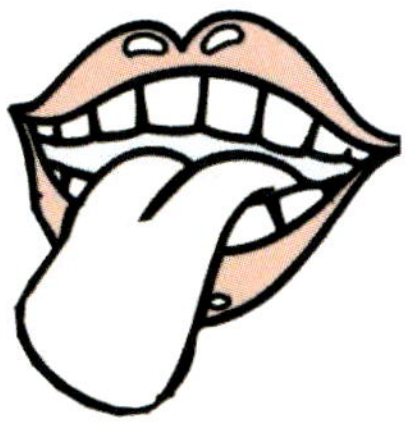

Hans sagt: 'Zeig mir das Kinn
Und den Finger auch!'
Hans sagt: 'Zeig mir das Knie
Und den Rücken auch!'
Hans sagt: 'Zeig mir das Herz
Und die Arme auch!'
Hans sagt: 'Zeig mir das Bein sofort
Und die Füße auch!'

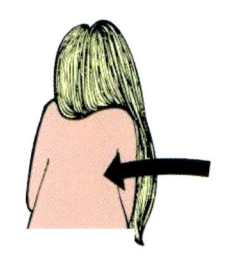

Der Körper

Volkslied
...Brüderlein

Brüderlein, komm tanz mit mir,
Beide Hände reich' ich dir!
Einmal hin, einmal her,
Brüderlein, das ist nicht schwer!

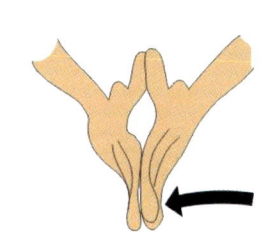

Mit den Händen, klip, klip, klap!
Mit den Füßen, trip, trip, trap!
Einmal hin, einmal her,
Brüderlein, das ist nicht schwer!

Mit dem Köpfchen, nick, nick, nick!
Mit dem Fingerchen, tick, tick, tick!
Einmal hin, einmal her,
Brüderlein, das ist nicht schwer!

Brüderlein, komm tanz mit mir,
Beide Hände reich' ich dir!
Einmal hin, einmal her,
Brüderlein, das ist nicht schwer!

Mit den Ohren, hör, hör, hör!
Mit der Nase, schnief, schnief, schnief!
Einmal hin, einmal her,
Brüderlein, das ist nicht schwer!

Mit den Beinen, spring, spring, spring!
Mit den Knien, beug, beug, beug!
Einmal hin, einmal her,
Brüderlein, das ist nicht schwer!

Brüderlein, komm tanz mit mir,
Beide Hände reich' ich dir!
Einmal hin, einmal her,
Brüderlein, das ist nicht schwer!

Die Kleidung

	ein Hut — hat		eine Schuluniform — school uniform
	eine Hose — trousers		ein Schottenrock — kilt
	ein Mantel — coat		Sportschuhe — trainers
	ein Pulli — pullover		Schuhe — shoes
	ein Blazer — blazer		Socken — socks
	Handschuhe — gloves		ein Schal — scarf
	ein T-Shirt — a tee shirt		eine Krawatte — tie
	Shorts — shorts		ein Kleid — dress
	eine Jacke — jacket		ein Hemd — shirt
	eine Strumpfhose — tights		ein Rock — skirt

Copyright Carole Nicoll 2005

Die Kleidung

Gespräch

Was trägst du?
Einen grünen Pulli.
Was trägst du?
Eine schwarze Hose.

Beschreibe deine Schuluniform.
Ich trage eine graue Hose, eine blaue Jacke und eine schwarz-gelbe Krawatte.
Ah! Wie schlimm!

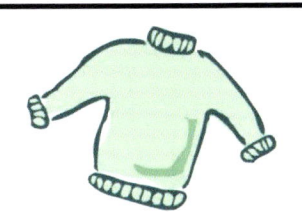

Lied... Die Waschmaschine

Was ist denn in der Waschmaschine?
Ein grüner Rock, ein grüner Rock!
Was ist denn in der Waschmaschine?
Ein grüner Rock von Omi.

Ein gelbes Kleid.
Ein roter Schal.
Ein blauer Hut.
Stinkige Socken!

Reim ...Der Storch

Eins, zwei, drei, vier, fünf.
Der Storch hat rote Strümpf.
Der Frosch, der hat kein Haus,
Und du bist raus!

Volkslied ...Mein Hut

Mein Hut, der hat drei Ecken.
Drei Ecken hat mein Hut,

Und hätt' er nicht drei Ecken,
So wär's auch nicht mein Hut!

Die Kleidung

bügeln — to iron	**ein Männlein** — a little man
waschen — to wash	**ein Mäntelein** — a little coat
ein Pilz — a mushroom	**eine Kappe** — a cap
ein Mann — a man	**ein Käppelein** — a little cap

Volkslied... Zeigt her eure Füße

Zeigt her eure Füße, zeigt her eure Schuh,
Und sieh den fleißigen Waschfrauen zu!
Sie waschen, sie waschen, sie waschen den ganzen Tag! (x2)
Sie bügeln, sie bügeln, sie bügeln den ganzen Tag! (x2)

Volkslied ...Ein Männlein steht im Walde

Ein Männlein steht im Walde,
Ganz still und stumm.
Es hat von lauter Purpur ein
Mäntelein um.
Sagt, wer mag das Männlein sein,
Das da steht im Wald allein,
Mit dem purpurroten Mäntelein.

Das Männlein steht im Walde
auf einem Bein.
Es hat auf seinem Haupte
Schwarz Käpplein klein.
Sagt, wer mag das Männlein sein,
Das da steht im Wald allein,
Mit dem kleinen
schwarzen Käppelein.

Copyright Carole Nicoll 2005

Die Stadt

 **ein Verkehrsamt**	*a Tourist Office*
 **eine Polizeiwache**	*a police station*
 **eine Drogerie**	*a chemist*
 **ein Markt**	*a market*
 **ein Café**	*a café*
 **ein Sportzentrum**	*a sports centre*
 **eine Bank**	*a bank*
 **eine Post**	*a Post Office*
 **eine Bäckerei**	*a bakery*
 **Toiletten**	*toilets*
 **ein Kino**	*a cinema*
 **rechts**	*to the right*
 **links**	*to the left*
 **geradeaus**	*straight on*

Gespräch 2

Wo wohnst du?

Ich wohne in Aberdeen in Nordschottland.

Ist Aberdeen eine Stadt oder ein Dorf?

Es ist eine Stadt.

Was kann man in Aberdeen machen?

Es gibt eine Eishalle, ein Sportzentrum und viele Geschäfte.

Das ist aber toll!

Copyright Carole Nicoll 2005

Die Stadt

ein Dorf	*a village*	 **eine Stadt**	*a town*
 **ein Supermarkt**	*a supermarket*	 **ein Bahnhof (DB)**	*a railway*
 **ein Stadion**	*a stadium*	 **ein Schwimmbad**	*a swimming pool*
 **ein Park**	*a park*	 **eine Disco**	*a disco*
 **ein Krankenhaus**	*a hospital*	 **ein Eishalle**	*a skating rink*
 **ein Flughafen**	*an airport*	 **eine Kirche**	*a church*
 **ein Museum**	*a museum*	 **ein Rummelplatz**	*a fairground*
ein Einkaufszentrum	*a shopping centre*	 **eine Brücke**	*a bridge*
ein Laden	*a shop*	 **eine Bibliothek**	*a library*
 **ein Theater**	*a theatre*	**eine Schule**	*a school*

Die Stadt 46

Gespräch

Entschuldigung! Wie komme ich zur Bank, bitte?

Geh nach rechts, geh nach links und immer geradeaus!

Danke! Tschüss.

Lied...Wie komme ich am besten..?

Wie komme ich am besten zur Bank, bitte schön? (x2)
Geh nach rechts, dann
geh nach links, dann
geh geradeaus und da ist sie!
Vielen Dank!

Wie komme ich am besten zur Post, bitte schön? (x2)
Geh nach rechts, dann
geh nach links, dann
geh geradeaus und da ist sie!
Vielen Dank!

Wie komme ich am besten zum Markt, bitte schön? (x2)
Geh nach rechts, dann
geh nach links, dann
geh geradeaus und da ist er!

Wie komme ich am besten zum Park, bitte schön? (x2)
Geh nach rechts, dann
geh nach links, dann
geh geradeaus und da ist er!
Vielen Dank!

Franzözisches Volkslied

Auf der Brücke von Avignon.
Laßt uns tanzen. Laßt uns tanzen!
Auf der Brücke von Avignon.
Laßt uns tanzen rund herum!

Englische Volkslied

Londons Brücke hat ein Loch,
Hat ein Loch. Hat ein Loch.
Rund ums Loch, da steht sie noch.
Meine Dame!

Copyright Carole Nicoll 2005

Der Zoo

ein Tiger — *a tiger*	 ein Pinguin — *a penguin*
ein Löwe — *a lion*	 ein Delphin — *a dolphin*
 ein Pandabär — *a panda*	ein Kamel — *a camel*
 ein Hai — *a shark*	ein Zebra — *a zebra*
ein Stachelschwein — *a porcupine*	 ein Bär/ein Eisbär — *a bear/a polar bear*
 ein Affe — *a monkey*	ein Elefant — *an elephant*
ein Känguruh — *a kangaroo*	 ein Pelikan — *a pelican*
 ein Krokodil — *a crocodile*	ein Nilpferd — *a hippopotamus*
ein Pfau — *a peacock*	 eine Viper — *an adder*
ein Seehund — *a seal*	 eine Giraffe — *a giraffe*

Der Zoo

Gespräch

Was für Tiere findet man im Zoo?

Man findet Tiger und Pandabären im Zoo.

Ah! Welche Farbe haben sie?

Der Tiger ist schwarz und orange, und der Pandabär ist schwarz und weiß!

Lied...Wir gehen in den Zoo

E I O (ay ee oh) Wir gehen in den Zoo.
Da gibt es viel zu schauen
Bei Tigern und bei Pfauen.
E I O (ay ee oh) Wir gehen in den Zoo. (x 2)

    E I AU (ay ee ow) Der Elefant ist grau.
    Die Viper, die verschwindet schnell,
    Der Eisbär hat ein weißes Fell.
    E I AU (ay ee ow) Der Elefant ist grau.

E I EU (ay ee oy) Kamele fressen Heu.
Der Delphin liebt die Fischerei.
Und Nüsse mag der Papagei.
E I EU (ay ee oy) Kamele fressen Heu.

    E I AI (ay ee aye) Sehr hungrig ist der Hai.
    Stachelig ist das Stachelschwein.
    Das Krokodil schaut böse drein.
    E I AI (ay ee aye) Sehr hungrig ist der Hai.

E I OCH (ay ee och) Giraffen sind ganz hoch.
Der Panda bleibt in seinem Haus.
Der Pelikan fliegt hoch hinaus.
E I OCH (ay ee och) Giraffen sind ganz hoch.

    E I Q (ay ee coo) Weit springt das Känguruh.
    Der Affe nach Bananen greift.
    Das Zebra is schwarz-weiß gestreift.
    E I Q (ay ee coo) Weit springt das Känguruh.

E I Z (ay ee zet) Der Seehund ist kokett.
Der Löwe kommt aus Afrika.
Der Tukan aus Amerika.
E I Z (ay ee zet) Der Seehund ist kokett.

    E I O (ay ee oh) Wir waren heut' im Zoo.
    Da gab es viel zu schauen.
    Bei Tigern und bei Pfauen.
    E I O (ay ee oh) Wir waren heut' im Zoo.

Copyright Carole Nicoll 2005

Der Bauernhof 49

 **ein Ziegenbock** *a billy goat* **eine Geiß** *a female goat*	 **ein Schwan** *a swan*
ein Schaf *a sheep*	**ein Hahn** *a cockerel*
 **eine Ente** *a duck*	**ein Schwein** *a pig*
 **eine Gans** *a goose*	**eine Biene** *a bee*
 **ein Fuchs** *a fox*	**eine Spinne** *a spider*
 **ein Igel** *a hedgehog*	 **ein Kleeblatt** *a clover leaf*
ein Vogel *a bird*	**ein Frosch** *a frog*
 **eine Pute** **eine Putthenne** *a turkey*	 **ein Kuckuck** *a cuckoo*
ein Esel *a donkey*	**ein Huhn** *a chicken*
 **ein scharfer Zahn** *a sharp tooth*	 **eine Kuh** *a cow*

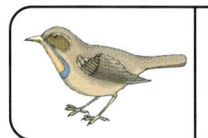

Copyright Carole Nicoll 2005

Der Bauernhof 50

Volkslied... Alle meine Entchen

Alle meine Entchen,
schwimmen auf dem See.
Köpfchen in das Wasser,
Schwänzchen in
die Höh'!

Witz

Was ist der Unterschied zwischen einem afrikanischen Elefant und einem asiatischen Elefant?
Ich weiß nicht!
10,000 Kilometer!
(Zehntausend Kilometer)

Gespräch

Was ist dein Lieblingstier im Zoo?
Mein Lieblingstier ist der Elefant!
Warum?
Weil er groß und stark ist, aber auch sehr gemütlich!
Was sind deine Lieblingstiere im Zoo?
Meine Lieblingstiere sind die Seehunde und die Affen.
Warum?
Weil sie so lustig sind!

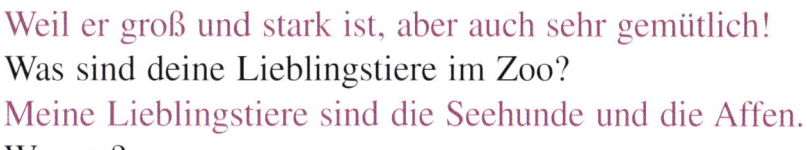

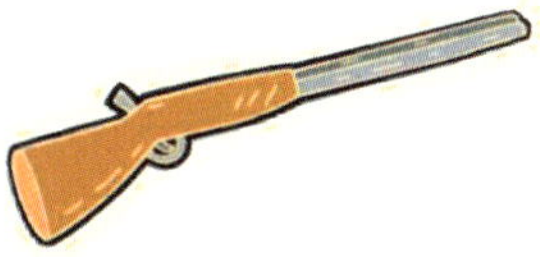

Volkslied... Fuchs, du hast die Gans gestohlen!

Fuchs, du hast die Gans gestohlen!
Gib sie wieder her! (x2)
Sonst wird dich der Jäger holen,
mit dem Schießgewehr. (x2)

Seine große lange Flinte
schießt auf dich den Schrot, (x2)
dass dich färbt die rote Tinte
und dann bist du tot! (x2)

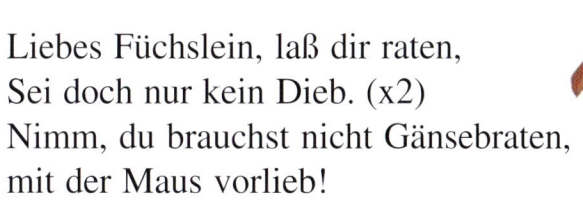

Liebes Füchslein, laß dir raten,
Sei doch nur kein Dieb. (x2)
Nimm, du brauchst nicht Gänsebraten,
mit der Maus vorlieb!

Zungenbrecher

Zehn Ziegen zogen zehn Zentner Zucker zum Zoo.

Copyright Carole Nicoll 2005

Der Bauernhof 51

	ein Käfer *a beetle*		**ein Fischer** *a fisherman*
	ein Storch *a stork*		**eine Birne** *a pear*
	eine Wanze *a bug*		**Blumen** *flowers*
	ein Hund *a dog*		**ein Bauer** *farmer (Old MacDonald)*
	ein Hase *a hare*		**eine Kappe** *a cap*
	ein Pilz *a mushroom*		**ein Baum** *a tree*
	eine Spitzmaus *a shrew*		**eine Amsel** *a blackbird*
	ein Marienkäfer *a ladybird*		**eine Schwalbe** *a swallow*
	ein Maikäfer *a big brown beetle*		**eine Flinte** *a shotgun*
	ein Jäger *a hunter*		**ein Traktor/ ein Trecker** *a tractor*

Copyright Carole Nicoll 2005

Der Bauernhof 52

Altes schottisches Volkslied
Old MacDonald hat ein Haus!

Old MacDonald hat ein Haus!
Hi a hi a ho!
Da schaut ein Hund zum Fenster raus!
Hi a hi a ho!
Der macht wau wau hier,
Und macht wau, wau, da!
Hier mal wau, da mal wau,
Überall macht's wau wau!
Old MacDonald hat ein Haus!
Hi a hi a ho!

Da schaut ein Pferd zum Fenster raus!
Ihh! Ihh!
Da schaut eine Maus zum Fenster raus!
Piep! Piep!
Da schaut eine Gans zum Fenster raus!
Quack! Quack!
Da schaut eine Kuh zum Fenster raus!
Muh! Muh!
Da schaut ein Huhn zum Fenster raus!
Gacker! Gacker!
Da schaut ein Schwein zum Fenster raus!
Schnauben…!

Volkslied ..Häschen in der Grube

Häschen in der Grube saß und schlief.
Armes Häschen bist du krank?
Dass du nicht mehr hüpfen kannst!
Häschen hüpf! Häschen hüpf! Häschen hüpf!

Häschen vor dem Hunde
hüte dich, hüte dich
hat gar einen scharfen Zahn
packt damit mein Häschen an
Häschen hüpf! Häschen hüpf! Häschen hüpf!

Copyright Carole Nicoll 2005

Der Bauernhof

Volkslied ...Der Kuckuck und der Esel

Der Kuckuck und der Esel,
die hatten einen Streit.
Wer wohl am besten sänge, (x2)
Zur schönen Maienzeit! (x2)

Der Kuckuck sprach 'Das kann ich!'
Und fing gleich an zu schrein.
'Ich aber kann es besser', (x2)
Fiel gleich der Esel ein. (x 2)

Das klang so schön und lieblich,
So schön von fern und nah.
Sie sangen alle beide (x2)!
Kuckuck, kuckuck. Ia, ia!
Kuckuck, kuckuck. Ia, ia!

Reim

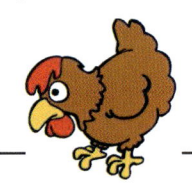

Sind die Hühner platt wie Teller,
War der Trecker wieder schneller!

Zungenbrecher

Schwimm, Schwan, schwimm!
Schwan weiß wie Schnee!
Schwimm, Schwan, schwimm!
Schwimm über den See!

Der Bauernhof 54

Reim

Eine kleine Spitzmaus,
Lief ums Rathaus,
Wollte sich was kaufen,
Hatte sich verlaufen!

Volkslied ...Widewidewenne

'Widewidewenne' heißt meine Putthenne!
'Kann Nicht Ruhn' heißt mein Huhn!
'Wackelschwanz' heißt meine Gans!
'Schwarz und Weiß' heißt meine Geiß!
'Kurze Bein' heißt mein Schwein!
'Widewidewenne' heißt meine Putthenne!

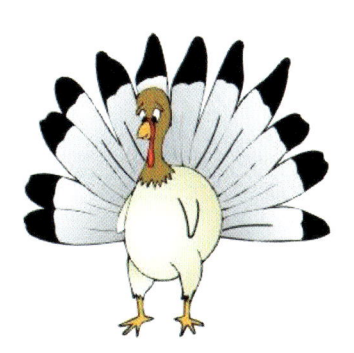

Zungenbrecher

Fischers Fritz fischt frische Fische!

Reim & Lied... Hopp Hopp Hopp

Hopp, hopp, hopp!
Pferdchen lauf Galopp!
Über Stock und über Steine,
Aber brich dir nicht die Beine!
Hopp, hopp, hopp. Hopp, hopp!
Pferdchen lauf Galopp!

Copyright Carole Nicoll 2005

Weihnachten 55

der Tannenbaum	xmas tree	die Kugel	bauble for tree
der Weihnachtsmann	Santa	die Glocke	the bell
der Schneemann	the snowman	der Dudelsack	the bagpipes
der Stern	the star	der Schlitten	the sleigh
das Geschenk	the present	das Bonbon	the sweet
die Kerze	the candle	die Laterne	the lantern
der Schnee	the snow	der Engel	the angel

Reim

Mein Wunch ist klein,
doch ist er wahr,
bleib recht gesund
im neuen Jahr!

Weihnachtslieder
...Laterne! Laterne!

Laterne! Laterne!
Sonne, Mond und Sterne!
Brenne auf mein Licht!
Brenne auf mein Licht!
Aber nur meine liebe Laterne nicht!

Copyright Carole Nicoll 2005

Weihnachten 56

Gespräch

Frohe Weihnachten und alles Gute für's Neue Jahr!

Volkslied ...Wir fahren nach Jerusalem!

Wir fahren nach Jerusalem,
Und wer kommt mit?
Das liegt nicht weit von Bethlehem.
Und du kommst mit!

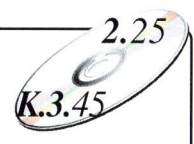

Schottische Volkslied ....Nehmt Abschied Brüder

Nehmt Abschied, Brüder, ungewiss
ist alle Wiederkehr.
Die Zukunft liegt in Finsternis
Und macht das Herz uns schwer.
Der Himmel wölbt sich übers Land
ade, auf Wiedersehen,
wir ruhen all' in Gottes Hand,
Lebt wohl, auf Wiedersehen!

Lebt wohl, auf Wiedersehen, Brüder.
Lebt wohl, auf Wiedersehen!
Wir ruhen all' in Gottes Hand,
Lebt wohl, auf Wiedersehen!

Weihnachtslieder

.... O Tannenbaum

O Tannenbaum, O Tannenbaum,
Wie grün sind deine Blätter! (x 2)
Du grünst nicht nur zur Sommerzeit,
Nein auch im Winter, wenn es schneit!
O Tannenbaum, O Tannenbaum,
Wie grün sind deine Blätter!

O Tannenbaum, O Tannenbaum,
Du kannst mir sehr gefallen! (x 2)
Wie oft hat nicht zur Weihnachtszeit,
Ein Baum von dir mich hoch erfreut!
O Tannenbaum, O Tannenbaum,
Du kannst mir sehr gefallen!

.... Stille Nacht

Stille Nacht, heilige Nacht,
alles schläft, einsam wacht,
nur das traute, hochheilige Paar,
holder Knabe im lockigen Haar.
schlaf in himmlischer Ruh,
schlaf in himmlischer Ruh!

Stille Nacht, heilige Nacht,
Hirten erst kundgemacht,
durch der Engel, Hallelujah,
tönt es laut von fern and nah.
Christ, der Retter, ist da,
Christ, der Retter, ist da.

Copyright Carole Nicoll 2005

Zahlen 1-60

1 eins	6 sechs	11 elf	16 sechzehn
2 zwei	7 sieben	12 zwölf	17 siebzehn
3 drei	8 acht	13 dreizehn	18 achtzehn
4 vier	9 neun	14 vierzehn	19 neunzehn
5 fünf	10 *zehn*	15 fünfzehn	20 *zwanzig*

21 einundzwanzig	22 zweiundzwanzig	23 dreiundzwanzig	24 vierundzwanzig
25 fünfundzwanzig	26 sechundzwanzig	27 siebenundzwanzig	28 achtundzwanzig
29 neunundzwanzig	30 *dreißig*		

31 einunddreißig	32 zweiunddreißig	33 dreiunddreißig	34 vierunddreißig
35 fünfunddreißig	36 sechsunddreißig	37 siebenunddreißig	38 achtunddreißig
39 neununddreißig	40 *vierzig*		

41 einundvierzig	42 zweiundvierzig	43 dreiundvierzig	44 vierundvierzig
45 fünfundvierzig	46 sechsundvierzig	47 siebenundvierzig	48 achtundvierzig
49 neunundvierzig	50 *fünfzig*		

51 einundfünfzig	52 zweiundfünfzig	53 dreiundfünfzig	54 vierundfünfzig
55 fünfundfünfzig	56 sechsundfünfzig	57 siebenundfünfzig	58 achtundfünfzig
59 neunundfünfzig	60 *sechzig*		

Copyright Carole Nicoll 2005

Zahlen 1-20

Gespräch

Hallo. Wie alt bis du?
Ich bin dreizehn. Und du?
Ich bin vierzehn!
Wie alt ist er?
Er ist neun.

Wie alt ist sie?
Sie ist zwei.
O sie ist süß, nicht wahr?
Ja! Bis morgen!

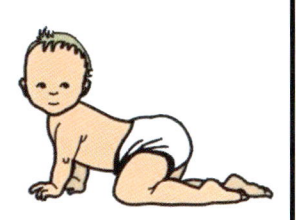

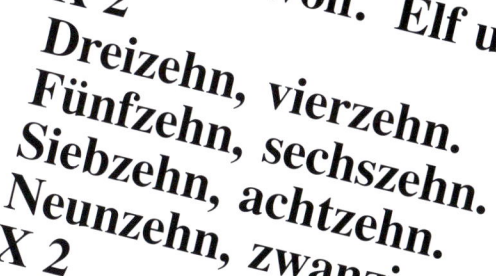

Lied

Eins, zwei, drei.
Vier, fünf, sechs.
Sieben, acht, neun und zehn.
Elf und zwölf.
X 2

...Eins, Zwei, Drei
Eins, zwei, drei.
Vier, fünf, sechs.
Elf und zwölf. (x 2)

Dreizehn, vierzehn.
Fünfzehn, sechszehn.
Siebzehn, achtzehn.
Neunzehn, zwanzig.
X 2

Reim

Eins, zwei, Polizei!
Drei, vier, Offizier!
Fünf, sechs, alte Hex!
Sieben, acht, gute Nacht!
Neun, zehn, auf Wiedersehen!

Mathe!

1 + 5 = 6
1 + 9 = 10
7 - 1 = 6
11 - 1 = 10
2 x 10 = 20
5 x 4 = 20
6 ÷ 2 = 3
Ach! Das kann ich nicht mehr!

Copyright Carole Nicoll 2005

Zahlen 61-100

61 einundsechzig	62 zweiundsechzig	63 dreiundsechzig	64 vierundsechzig
65 fünfundsechzig	66 sechundsechzig	67 siebenundsechzig	68 achtundsechzig
69 neunundsechzig	70 *siebzig*		

71 einundsiebzig	72 zweiundsiebzig	73 dreiundsiebzig	74 vierundsiebzig
75 fünfundsiebzig	76 sechsundsiebzig	77 siebenundsiebzig	78 achtundsiebzig
79 neunundsiebzig	80 *achtzig*		

81 einundachtzig	82 zweiundachtzig	83 dreiundachtzig	84 vierundachtzig
85 fünfundachtzig	86 sechsundachtzig	87 siebenundachtzig	88 achtundachtzig
89 neunundachtzig	90 *neunzig*		

91 einundneunzig	92 zweiundneunzig	93 dreiundneunzig	94 vierundneunzig
95 fünfundneunzig	96 sechsundneunzig	97 siebenundneunzig	98 achtundneunzig
99 neunundneunzig	100 *hundert*		

1000 *tausend*

200 zweihundert	203 zweihundertdrei	210 zweihundertzehn

10000 zehntausend	100000 hunderttausend	1000000 eine Million

Copyright Carole Nicoll 2005

Zahlen 10-100

60

Gespräch 1

Eh! Volker! Was ist deine Telefonnummer?
Meine Nummer? 70 61 73
Und du Peter?
70 76 81
Telefon für mich!
Nein für mich!

+ und
- weniger
x mal
= macht
÷ durch

Gespräch 2

Was ist das?
Das ist dreißig!
Was ist das?
Das ist sechzig!
Was macht eins und fünf?
Eins und fünf macht sechs.

Was macht zehn weniger eins?
Zehn weniger eins macht neun!
Was macht zwei mal zwei?
Zwei mal zwei macht vier!
Und zehn durch zwei?
Zehn durch zwei macht fünf!

Witz

Was hat acht Beine, zwei Räder und fährt sehr schnell?

Ich weiß nicht!

Eine Spinne auf einem Motorrad!

6,998,722

sechs Millionen neunhundertachtundneunzigtausendsiebenhundertzweiundzwanzig!

Copyright Carole Nicoll 2005

Grammatik

Dear Parent or Teacher.....
The following pages explain some basic grammar points. Knowledge of these will provide your child or pupils with the basic building blocks necessary to form sentences and thus progress further! Your guidance through this section will be of benefit to your child/pupils.

Grammatik

Word Order in German	**61**
How to say **'the'** in German	**62**
How to make words **plural** in German	**63**
How to say **'a'** or **'an'** in German	**64**
How to say **who possesses things** in German	**66**
Verbs - Pronouns	**67**
- The present tense	**68**
- Useful verbs	**69**
- Some irregular verbs	**70**
Adjectives - Describing things in German	**71**
How to say **'to the'** in German	**73**
Prepositions	**74**
Explaining cases	**75**
Explaining gender	**77**
Terms of Endearment 'lein' and 'chen'	**78**

Copyright Carole Nicoll 2005

How to use word order in German

Notice that we have two ways in German to say

"I have a cat in my house".

We can say

"Ich habe eine Katze in meinem Haus"

but the Germans like to begin with "in my house".

Look what happens when they do this!

"In meinem Haus **habe ich** eine Katze"

They do this very often. Here are some examples:-

In meinem Zimmer **gibt es** ein Bett

In my room there is a bed.

In meiner Schule **gibt es** ein Schwimmbad.

In my school there is a swimming pool.

How to say 'the' in German — 62

There are different words in German that mean the.

Here are some words meaning **the**, der die das and die

To start with let's look at der die and das

In German, nouns (things as well as people) are either **masculine**, **feminine** or **neuter**.

The word in front of the noun usually shows if that noun is **masculine**, **feminine** or **neuter**.

der shows that something is **masculine**.
die shows that something is **feminine**.
das shows that something is **neuter**.

When you learn a new word it is important to learn it with the **der**, **die** or **das** in front of it.

der is used before all **masculine** nouns.
die is used before all **feminine** nouns.
das is used before all **neuter** nouns.

Here are some masculine words you may already know.

| **der** Junge | **the** boy | **der** Wagen | **the** car |
| **der** Kuli | **the** pen | **der** Hund | **the** dog |

Here are some feminine words you may already know.

| **die** Frau | **the** woman | **die** Katze | **the** cat |
| **die** Nase | **the** nose | **die** Mutter | **the** mother |

Here are some neuter words you may already know.

| **das** Heft | **the** jotter | **das** Kleid | **the** dress |
| **das** Buch | **the** book | **das** Hemd | **the** shirt |

Copyright Carole Nicoll 2005

How to make words plural in German

Another word in German that means **the** is | die |

This is different from the other 'die' which shows that a word is feminine.

| die | is used before a plural noun. (Plural means more than one.)

In English we often put an **'s'** on the end of the word to make it plural.

e.g.   the pen   the pens
       der Kuli   **die** Kulis

In German too, an **'s'** is **sometimes** put on the end of the word to make it plural.

But very often an **'n'** or **'en'** is added in German to make a word plural

e.g.   der Zeh   **die** Zehen   the toes
       die Nase   **die** Nasen   the noses
       das Ohr   **die** Ohren   the ears

die Augen   the eyes

The difference in German is that you must remember to use | die | for **the** before a plural noun.

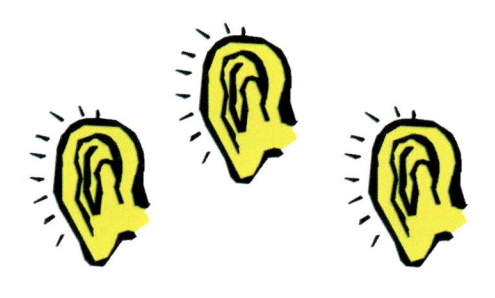

die Ohren

Copyright Carole Nicoll 2005

How to say 'a' or 'an'

We have already seen that in German nouns (things as well as people) are either **masculine**, **feminine** or **neuter**.

We have seen that when we want to say **the** in German we use **der** for masculine nouns (people or things), **die** for feminine nouns (people or things) and **das** for neuter nouns (people or things).

In the same way there are different words in German for **a** (or **an**).

These are **ein**, **eine** and **ein**
(Ein is used for both masculine and neuter nouns.)

ein for **masculine** people or things, e.g. **ein** Junge (a boy) **ein** Kuli (a pen)
eine for **feminine** people or things, e.g. **eine** Frau (a woman)
ein for neuter people or things, e.g. **ein** Mädchen (a girl) **ein** Heft (a jotter)

Here are some classroom words which are masculine.

ein Bleistift (a pencil)	**ein** Kuli (a pen)
ein Stuhl (a chair)	**ein** Computer (a computer)

Here are some classroom words which are **feminine**.

eine Tür (a door)
eine Tafel (a blackboard)

Here are some classroom words which are neuter.

ein Fenster (a window)	**ein** Heft (a jotter)
ein Buch (a book)	**ein** Mädchen (a girl)

Copyright Carole Nicoll 2005

How to say 'a' or 'an' — 65

Häuser

As we have already seen, when we want to say **the** referring to more than one thing we use **die**

e.g. **die** Kulis   **die** Häuser

No word is required for the plural of 'a'.

When we want to refer to more than one thing, we just say

Mädchen (girls)   Bücher (books)   Jungen (boys)   Augen (eyes)

Just as in English we say 'a house' but if there are more than one we say 'houses', so in German they say 'ein Haus' but 'Häuser' for more than one.

Notice

Mädchen

Ein for masculine and ein for neuter look alike. However, if we use them with 'ich habe' (I have) so that together with the noun (a brother, a dog), they become the object of the sentence, then the masculine 'ein' changes to 'einen'.

Ich habe **einen** Bruder   (I have a brother)
Ich habe **einen** Hund   (I have a dog)

but

Ich habe **ein** Haus   (I have a house)

Copyright Carole Nicoll 2005

How to say who possesses things — 66

We have already seen that in German nouns (things as well as people) are either **masculine**, **feminine** or **neuter**.

We have already seen that when we want to say **the** in German we use **der** for masculine people or things (e.g. der Hund), **die** for feminine people or things (e.g. die Frau), and **das** for neuter people or things (e.g. das Buch, das Mädchen).

We use **die** for plurals, e.g. **die** Kulis.   **die** Häuser.

We have also seen that when we want to say **a** (or **an**) we use **ein** before masculine nouns, **eine** before feminine nouns and **ein** before neuter nouns.

In the same way, we can use the words **my, your, his** and **her**.

These are called possessive adjectives because they show that something is **belonging** to somebody.

Look at the table below:

Masculine	Feminine	Neuter	Plural	English
der	die	das	die	the
ein	eine	ein		a/an
mein	meine	mein	meine	my
dein	deine	dein	deine	*your (familiar)
sein	seine	sein	seine	his
ihr	ihre	ihr	ihre	her

* This is used when referring to people who are familiar to you such as family, friends, children and also when referring to animals.

Here are some examples with some of the words you already know.

mein Kuli *(my pen)*, **meine** Schwester *(my sister)*, **mein** Haus *(my house)*, **meine** Tiere *(my animals)*.

dein Bruder *(your brother)*, **deine** Mutter *(your mother)*, **dein** Buch *(your book)*, **deine** Augen *(your eyes)*.

sein Vater *(his father)*, **seine** Katze *(his cat)*, **sein** Pferd *(his horse)*, **seine** Ohren *(his ears)*.

ihr Wagen *(her car)*, **ihre** Tante *(her aunt)*, **ihr** Bett **(her bed)**, **ihre** Füße *(her feet)*.

Copyright Carole Nicoll 2005

Verbs - pronouns

How to say who is doing the action of the verb

Here are the English Personal Pronouns:

I. You. He. She. It. One.
*These are all **singular** as they only refer to one person.*

We. You. They.
*These are all **plural** as they refer to more than one person.*

Below are the German Personal Pronouns:

ich	*I*	
du	*You*	(familiar) (Use this when referring to children, friends, family and animals)
er	*He*	
sie	*She*	
es	*It*	
man	*One*	This is used more frequently in German than in English.

wir	*We*	
ihr	*You*	Use this when referring to more than one person you know well
Sie	*You*	This can be used in two different ways. 1. When referring to a person you respect, such as a teacher, or an adult you don't know well. 2. When you are referring to more than one person.
sie	*They*	Use this when referring to more than one person or thing.

Verbs - the present tense | 68

The Present Tense

The Present Tense is the tense you use when you are referring to something that is happening **now.**

Before you use a verb you must take the **en** off the infinitive (the whole verb) and add the ending you need.

To form the present tense of any regular verb you take the **stem** of the infinitive and add … **e st t en t en en** as follows.

ich spiele	I play. I am playing. I do play
du spielst	You (familiar) play. You are playing. You do play
er/sie/es/man spielt er = he sie = she es = it man = one	He/She/It/One plays. He/She/It/One is playing. He/She/It/One does play.
wir spielen	We play. We are playing. We do play.
ihr spielt	You (plural informal) play. You are playing. You do play.
Sie spielen	You (singular or plural formal) play. You are playing. You do play.
sie spielen	They play. They are playing. They do play.

Copyright Carole Nicoll 2005

Some useful verbs in German

Here are some useful verbs in German.

These are all infinitives.

singen	*to sing*
machen	*to do*
spielen	*to play*
sagen	*to say*
heißen	*to be called*
sprechen	*to speak*
telefonieren	*to phone*
wohnen	*to live*
rennen	*to race*
besuchen	*to visit, to see round*
hören	*to listen to*
lieben	*to adore, love*
sammeln	*to collect*

Some irregular verbs 70

We have already met some **useful** verbs that follow a regular pattern. Here are five common **irregular** verbs, which do not follow a regular pattern, so they must be learnt individually!

haben	to have
ich habe	I have
du hast	You have
er hat sie hat es hat man hat	He/She/ It/One has
wir haben	We have
ihr habt	You have
Sie haben	You have
sie haben	They have

sein	to be
ich bin	I am
du bist	You are
er ist sie ist es ist man ist	He/She/ It/One is
wir sind	We are
ihr seid	You are
Sie sind	You are
sie sind	They are

können	*to be able*
ich kann	I can
du kannst	You can
er kann sie kann es kann man kann	He/She/ It/One can
wie können	We can
ihr könnt	You can
Sie können	You can
sie können	They can

gehen	*to go*
ich gehe	*I go*
du gehst	*You go*
er geht sie geht es geht man geht	*He/She/* *It/One goes*
wir gehen	*We go*
ihr geht	*You go*
Sie gehen	*You go*
sie gehen	*They go*

fahren	*to travel*
ich fahre	*I go*
du fährst	*You go*
er fährt sie fährt es fährt man fährt	*He/She/* *It/One goes*
wir fahren	*We go*
ihr fahrt	*You go*
Sie fahren	*You go*
sie fahren	*They go*

Notice that the formal you, Sie, in German always has a capital S. Gehen is only used if we are going anywhere on foot.
Notice that in German we have two verbs of going. Fahren must be used if we are going by any mechanised transport.

Copyright Carole Nicoll 2005

Adjectives (71)

Words that describe things are called adjectives.
Here are some German adjectives.

neu *new*	**alt** *old*
frech *naughty*	**jung** *young*
schlecht *bad*	**teuer** *expensive*
gut *good*	**billig** *cheap*
hässlich *ugly*	**schön** *beautiful*
hübsch *pretty*	**klein** *little*
lang *long*	**dick** *fat*
sehr groß *huge*	**groß** *big / tall*

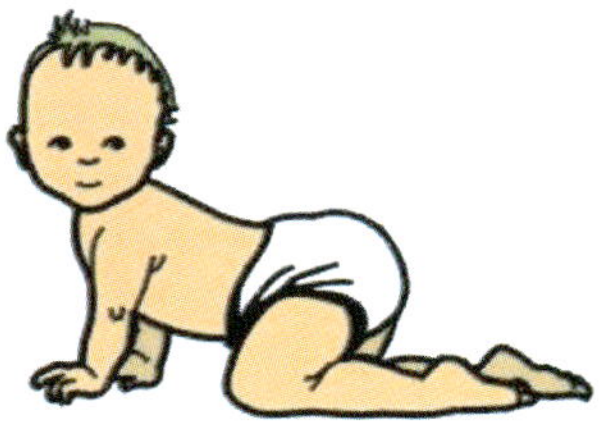

Adjectives

In German, the easiest way to describe anything is to say:-

The boy is **tall.**	Der Junge ist **groß.**
The elephant is **grey.**	Der Elefant ist **grau.**
The house is **old.**	Das Haus ist **alt.**
The sky is **blue.**	Der Himmel ist **blau.**

In this way, the adjective is freestanding and always remains the same.

However when the adjective is in front of a noun the ending may change, e.g.

I have **blond** hair.	Ich habe **blonde** Haare.
He has **blue** eyes.	Er hat **blaue** Augen.
She has **long** hair.	Sie hat **lange** Haare.

Copyright Carole Nicoll 2005

Saying 'to the' in German — 73

Saying 'to' a place in a town - in German

To say you are going 'to the' in German you say **zum** or **zur.**

Zum is used with **masculine** or **der** nouns.

Zum is used with **neuter** or **das** nouns.

Zur is used with **feminine** or **die** nouns.

Here are some examples:-

I'm going to the market.	Ich gehe **zum** Markt.
I'm going to the post office.	Ich gehe **zur** Post.
I'm going to the swimming pool.	Ich gehe **zum** Schwimmbad.

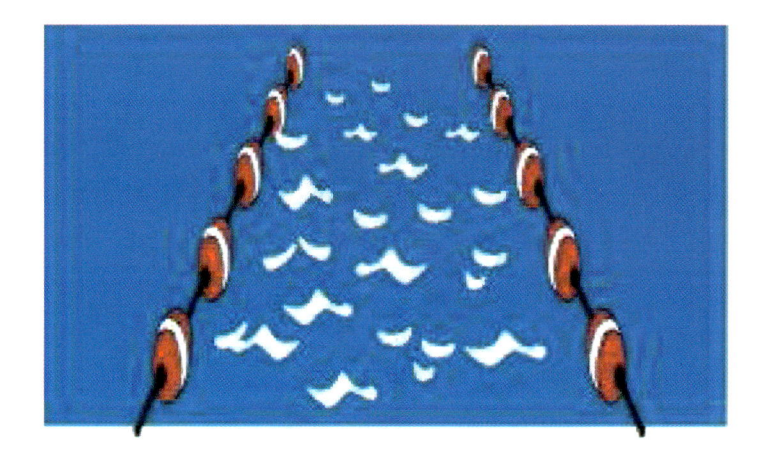

If you want to say **'to' a country** use **nach** e.g.

nach Deutschland   **to** Germany

Copyright Carole Nicoll 2005

Prepositions

74

hinter — *behind*	**auf** — *on*
vor — *in front of*	**zwischen** — *between*
unter — *under*	**in** — *in*
die Maus — *the mouse*	**der Kasten** — *the box*

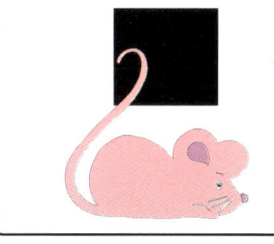

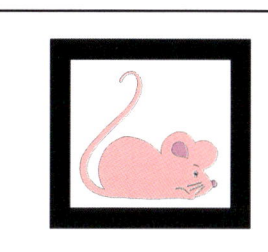

die Maus ist hinter dem Kasten.
The mouse is behind the box.

die Maus ist vor dem Kasten.
The mouse is in front of the box.

die Maus ist unter dem Kasten.
The mouse is under the box.

die Maus ist auf dem Kasten.
The mouse is on the box.

die Maus ist zwischen den Kästen.
The mouse is between the boxes.

die Maus ist in dem Kasten.
The mouse is in the box.

At the end of this grammar section there are some tables explaining the CASES in German.

	Masculine	Feminine	Neuter	Plural
Dative	dem	der	dem	den

Copyright Carole Nicoll 2005

Explaining Cases

Explaining what Cases are.

The different endings at the end of many words in German show the job these words are doing in the sentence and make the meaning clear. You have seen different endings on verbs (page 68) showing you the endings for the present tense and which pronoun matches with that particular ending.
The job a noun does in a sentence is made clear by the "cases" in German. Words like "a, the, my, your, his, her, or adjectives etc.," standing right next to the nouns in these cases must match them and so their endings change to suit the case of the noun.

The Nominative Case.
The subject is the person or thing that does the action.
This case is used for the subject of the sentence.
Der Man wohnt hier. The man lives here.
The man is the subject of the sentence, therefore **DER** is used (see table on following page...)

The Accusative Case.
The direct object is the person or thing affected by the action. This case is used for the direct object of the sentence.
Ich habe *den* Kuli. I have the pen.
The pen is the object of the sentence, therefore DEN is used.
(see table on following page...)

The Dative Case
The person or thing to or for whom something is done. This is used for the indirect object of the sentence.
Ich zeige *dem* Lehrer die Arbeit. I show the work to the teacher.
The teacher is the indirect object as he is having the work shown to him, therefore **DEM** is used (see table on following page...)

The dative case is also used after many prepositions (see page 74...)
Die Maus ist **hinter dem** Kasten. The mouse is **behind the** box.
The dative, in this case **DEM,** is used **after** the preposition **hinter.**
(see table on following page...)

Copyright Carole Nicoll 2005

Explaining Cases

76

Explaining what Cases are continued.

The Genitive Case
This case is used when English uses 'of' or an apostrophe to indicate 'belonging to'.
That is the brother's book. Das ist das Buch des Bruders.

Table to help you decide whether to use der, die, das or die when using THE.

THE	Masculine	Feminine	Neuter	Plural
Nominative	der	die	das	die
Accusative	den	die	das	die
Genitive	des	der	des	der
Dative	dem	der	dem	den

Table to help you decide whether to use ein, eine or ein, when using A or AN.

A or AN	Masculine	Feminine	Neuter
Nominative	ein	eine	ein
Accusative	einen	eine	ein
Genitive	eines	einer	eines
Dative	einem	einer	einem

Table to help you decide whether to use kein, keine, kein or keine when using NOT or NO.

NOT or NO	Masculine	Feminine	Neuter	Plural
Nominative	kein	keine	kein	keine
Accusative	keinen	keine	kein	keine
Genitive	keines	keiner	keines	keiner
Dative	keinem	keiner	keinem	keinen

Ich habe keinen Bruder. I don't have a brother. Bruder is the direct object, therefore the Accusative case must be used.

Ich habe keine Bücher. I don't have any books.
Bücher has an umlaut added over the u to make it plural - (see other plurals page 63)

Copyright Carole Nicoll 2005

Explaining Gender

Explaining Gender.
All German nouns belong to one of three 'genders' or groups - masculine, feminine and neuter. Which gender a noun belongs to is not always logical. The word for 'girl' is das Mädchen which is neuter! The only way to get it right is to **learn the word for THE** (der die or das) **with the noun.**

Following the rules below may help you.
Nouns are always **masculine** if they come under the following headings or groups…

days	der Samstag	*Saturday*
months	der Januar	*January*
seasons	der Herbst	*Autumn*
males	der Mann	*man*
makes of car	der BMW	*BMW*
most nouns ending in er	der Computer	*computer*

Nouns are always **feminine** if they come under the following headings or groups…

most females	die Tante	*aunt*
numbers	die Sieben	*seven*
most nouns ending in e	die Katze	*cat*
nouns ending in ei	die Bäckerei	*bakery*
nouns ending in ie	die Drogerie	*chemist's*
nouns ending in ung	die Rechnung	*bill*
nouns ending in heit	die Krankheit	*illness*
nouns ending in keit	die Höflichkeit	*information*
nouns ending in schaft	die Landschaft	*countryside*

Nouns are always **neuter** if they come under the following headings or groups…

infinitives used as nouns	das Tanzen	*dancing*
nouns ending in chen	das Mädchen	*girl*
nouns ending in um	das Museum	*museum*

Note
To confuse things totally, some words have more than one gender!
e.g. die See   sea
     der See   lake

Compound Nouns (big words) are when two or more nouns are joined together.
e.g. der Bus + die Fahrerin = die Busfahrerin (female bus driver)
The gender of these words is always the same as the gender of the noun at the END of it.

Copyright Carole Nicoll 2005

Terms of Endearment

Terms of Endearment

If **lein** or **chen** is added to the word it acts as a 'term of endearment'.
The noun can be translated as 'dear' or 'little'.
A noun with these endings always becomes **NEUTER** e.g.

der Bruder	brother	das Brüderlein	dear/ little brother
der Kopf	head	das Köpfchen	little head
die Kappe	cap	das Käpplein	little cap

These are often found in nursery rhymes and songs for children.
Other examples are
Füchslein, Schneeflöckchen, Säcklein, Blümchen, Fingerchen.

das Brüderlein

das Füchslein

das Hündchen

das Käpplein

das Kätzchen

CD 1 Track Listings 1-25

Grüße *Greetings*
1. Reim 'Wie heißt du?
   Rap 'Guten Tag! Gute Nacht!' **K.1.26**

Tage *Days*
2. Gespräch
   Lied 'Montag, Dienstag, Mittwoch.' **K.1.27**

Der Körper *The Body*
3. Gespräch
4. Lied 'Kopf, Schultern, Knie und Zehen.' **K.1.28**
   Lied 'Schwuppi Wuppi' **K.1.29**

Das Café *The Café*
5. Gespräch
   Lied 'Das Café' **K.1.30**
6. Lied 'Wir haben Hunger' **K.1.31**

Im Klassenzimmer *In the Classroom*
7. Gespräch
   Song 'Das Klassenzimmer' **K.1.32**

Das Wetter *The Weather*
8. Gespräch
   Lied 'Das Wetter' **K.1.33**
9. Reim
   Volkslied 'Schneewalzer' **K.1.34**

Mein Geburtstag *My Birthday*
10. Gespräch
    Lied 'Ersten, zweiten, dritten' **K.1.35**
11. Lied 'Zum Geburtstag viel Glück' **K.1.36**

Tiere *Animals*
12. Gespräch
    Rap 'Hast du ein Haustier?' **K.1.37**
13. Gespräch
    Lied 'Wir gehen in den Zoo' **K.1.38**
14. Volkslied 'Fuchs, du hast die Gans gestohlen!' **K.1.39**
15. Reim & Volkslied 'Alle meine Entchen'

Die Zeit *The Time*
16. Gespräch
    Lied 'Wie spät ist es?' **K.1.40**
17. Reim and Volkslied 'Große Uhren'

Sportarten *Sports*
18. Gespräch
    Rap 'Sportarten' **K.1.41**

Das Alphabet *The Alphabet*
19. Gespräch
    Lied 'ABC' **K.1.42**

Monate *Months*
20. Gespräch
    Lied 'Januar, Februar.' **K.1.43**

Die Stadt *The Town*
21. Gespräch
    Lied 'Wie komme ich am besten?' **K.1.44**

Zahlen *Numbers 1 - 20*
22. Gespräch
    Lied 'Eins zwei drei' **K.1.45**
23. Reim 'Eins, zwei, Polizei!'

Farben *Colours*
24. Gespräch
    Lied 'Welche Farbe ist das?' **K.1.46**

Weihnachten *Xmas*
25. Gespräch
    Volkslied 'Nehmt Abschied'

K = Karaoke version of track

Copyright Carole Nicoll 2005

CD 2 Track Listings 1-31

Grüße *Greetings*
1. Gespräch 1
   Gespräch 2
2. Lied 'Gute Nacht, Mädchen' **K.3.34**
3. Gespräch 3

Der Körper *The Body*
4. Lied. 'Hans sagt.' **K.3.35**
5. Volkslied 'Brüderlein' **K.3.36**

Die Kleidung *Clothes*
6. Volkslied 'Mein Hut'
7. Gespräch
7. Lied 'Die Waschmachine' **K.3.37**
8. Volkslied 'Zeigt her eure Füße'
9. Reim 'Der Storch'
10. Volkslied 'Ein Männlein steht im Walde'

Wie siehst du aus? *What do you look like?*
11. Gespräch
    Lied 'Wie siehst du aus?' **K.3.38**
12. Volkslied 'Spannenlanger Hansel'
13. Zungenbrecher. 'Die Wichtel'

Die Familie *The Family*
14. Gespräch
    Lied 'Bruder, Vater, Großvater.' **K.3.39**
15. Reim & Volkslied 'Es war eine Mutter' **K.3.40**

Verkehrsmittel *Means of Transport*
16. Gespräch
    Lied 'Die Reifen am Bus'
17. Lied 'Meine Oma fährt Motorrad'
18. Volkslied 'Sag mir, was machen die Matrosen'
19. Volkslied 'Mein Bonnie'

Farben *Colours*
20. Gespräch
    Lied 'Lieblingsfarbe' **K.3.41**
21. Reim 'An der Ampel'
    Lied 'Was ist gelb?' **K.3.42**
22. Reim 'Das Gras ist grün'
    Volkslied 'Grün Grün Grün' **K.3.43**

Das Alphabet *The Alphabet*
23. Rap 'Die Vokale A E I O U' **K.3.44**
24. Reim 'ABCDE'
    Volkslied 'ABC Die Katze lief im Schnee!'

Weihnachten *Xmas*
25. Volkslied 'Wir fahren nach Jerusalem!' **K.3.45**
26. Weihnachtslied 'Stille Nacht' **K.3.46**
27. Volkslied 'Laterne! Laterne!'
28. Weihnachtslied 'O Tannenbaum' **K.3.47**

Im Klassenzimmer *In the Classroom*
29. Gespräch
30. Lied 'Von den blauen Bergen'

Das Café *The Café*
31. Reim ''Kein Wein', sagt das Schwein'

K = Karaoke version of track

Copyright Carole Nicoll 2005

CD 3 Track Listings 1-48

Jahreszeiten *Seasons*
1. Gespräch
2. Volkslied 'Summ summ summ!'
3. Volkslied 'Kuckuck! Kuckuck!'
4. Volkslied 'Alle Vögel sind schon da'
5. Reim 'Gelbes Blatt, falle ab.'
6. Volkslied 'Ja ja ja! Der Sommertag ist da!'
7. Reim 'Ru Ru Risch'

Mein Geburtstag *My Birthday*
8. Gespräch
   Lied 'Wer im Januar' K.3.48

Tiere *Animals*
9. Reim & Lied 'Hopp Hopp Hopp!'
10. Zungenbrecher 'Schwimm, Schwan, schwimm'
11. Lied 'Old MacDonald hat ein Haus'
12. Zungenbrecher 'Fischers Fritz'
13. Volkslied 'Häschen in der Grube'
14. Reim 'Eine kleine Spitzmaus'
    Volkslied 'Widewidewenne'
15. Reim 'Der Trecker'
16. Volkslied 'Der Kuckuck und der Esel'

Das Wetter *The Weather*
17. Gespräch
18. Reim 'Wenn die Sonne scheint'
    Lied 'Es regnet, es regnet'
19. Reim 'Imse Wimse Spinne'
20. Reim 'Schneeflöckchen'

Der Zoo *The Zoo*
21. Gespräch
22. Witz 'Elefant'
23. Zungenbrecher 'Zehn Ziegen'

Die Zeit *The Time*
24. Gespräch
25. Reim 'Morgens früh um sechs'

Sportarten *Sports*
26. Gespräch

Die Stadt *The Town*
27. Gespräch
28. Volkslied 'Auf der Brücke von Avignon'
29. Volkslied 'Londons Brücke'

Zahlen *Numbers*
30. Gespräch 1
31. Gespräch 2
32. Witz 'Was hat acht Beine?'

In meinem Schlafzimmer *In My Bedroom*
33. Gespräch
    Volkslied 'Schlaf, Kindchen, schlaf!'
    Reim 'Maikäfer flieg!'

K = Karaoke version of track

Note: tracks 34 to 48 are karaoke versions of songs from CDs 2 and 3

K.34. Lied 'Gute Nacht, Mädchen'
K.35. Lied. 'Hans sagt.'
K.36. Volkslied 'Brüderlein'
K.37. Lied 'Die Waschmachine'
K.38. Lied 'Wie siehst du aus?'
K.39. Lied 'Bruder, Vater, Großvater.'
K.40. Reim & Volkslied 'Es war eine Mutter'
K.41. Lied 'Lieblingsfarbe'
K.42. Lied 'Was ist gelb?'
K.43. Volkslied 'Grün Grün Grün'
K.44. Rap 'Die Vokale A E I O U'
K.45. Volkslied 'Wir fahren nach Jerusalem!'
K.46. Weihnachtslied 'Stille Nacht'
K.47. Weihnachtslied 'O Tannenbaum'
K.48. Lied 'Wer im Januar'

Copyright Carole Nicoll 2005

CD 1 Auf Englisch! In English!

Grüße *Greetings*
1. Rhyme
What are you called? I'm called Udo.
What is he called? He's called Pierre.
What is she called? She is called Marie.
Thanks Peter! See you later!

Rap Good Day! Good Night!
Good Day! Good Night!
Good Morning! Good Night!
Good Evening! Good Night!
How are you? Not bad!
Hello! What is your name?
I'm called Carla!
Goodbye!
See you later!
Goodbye, Mrs Smith!

Tage *Days*
2. Conversation
What day is it today? Today is Monday.
And yesterday? Yesterday was Sunday.
And tomorrow? Tomorrow is therefore Tuesday!
Aaah! What next!

Song Monday. Tuesday. Wednesday.
Monday. Tuesday. Wednesday.
Thursday. Friday. Saturday.
Tell me what is still missing?
Oh yes! Sunday!

Der Körper *The Body*
3. Conversation
What is that? That is my head!
What is that? That is my nose!
What is that? That is my ear!

Song Head, Shoulders, Knees and Toes.
Head, shoulders, knees and toes. Knees and toes!
Eyes, ears, nose, mouth and chin!
Head, shoulders, knees and toes. Knees and toes!

4. Song Hokey Cokey
We put the right hand in.
The right hand out.
In, out, shake it out.
We do the Oki Koki,
And we turn around.
That's how it is done!
Oh! Oki Koki! (x 3)
That is how it is done!
We put the left foot in…
We put the right ear in…
We put the bottom in…

Das Café *The Café*
5. Conversation
Waiter!
Good Evening! Can I help you?
Yes, please.
What do you want?
I want a coffee, please.
And you? What would you like?
I would like a coke, please.
Ok, my pleasure. Thank you.
Enjoy your drinks!
Waiter! The bill, please!
Thank you!
My goodness! That was expensive!

Song The Café
Good Evening! What would you like, sir?
I would like a tea, and a coffee, a hamburger,
a doughnut, beer for my wife, a lemonade
as well, and ham on toast for me!

6. Song I'm Hungry!
I'm hungry, hungry, hungry. I'm thirsty!
Bring the water and bring the sausages!
I'm hungry, hungry, hungry. I'm thirsty!
Bring the juice and bring the sausage!
Bring the beer and bring the sausage!
Bring the wine and bring the sausage!

Im Klassenzimmer *In the Classroom*
7. Conversation
What is that? That is a computer.
What have you got in your pencil case?
In my pencil case there is a pen, a sharpener,
a rubber and some scissors.

Song The Classroom
A pen is in my pencil case,
A pencil and a ruler
And I also have some scissors,
a sharpener, a rubber.
What do I have? Where? (x2)
What do I have in my pencil case? (x2)
A jotter is in the rucksack
and I have homework, too,
a book, a small calculator,
some glue and sellotape, too!
In the classroom there are two computers,
A window and also a door.
Chairs, tables and a white board.
A teacher and a rubbish bin, too!

Das Wetter *The Weather*
8. Conversation
What is the weather like in Africa?
In Africa it is hot and sunny, but sometimes it rains.
What is the weather like in Iceland?
In Iceland it is cold, but sometimes it is hot.

Song What is the weather like?
What is the weather like?
It is hot! Today the sun is shining!
It is hot!
What is the weather like?
It is cold! It is snowing and it is raining!
It is cold.
What is the weather like?
It is windy and chilly. It is also cloudy.
Windy and chilly.
What is the weather like?
It is bad and it is very foggy.
What a day!

9. Rhyme
White as chalk. Light as fluff.
Soft as silk. Moist as foam.
The snow! The snow!
On every tree!

Folksong The Snow Waltz
When in spring flowers bloom
and the trees become green.
When a bird sings in the wood,
The summer sun will soon be shining!
When the autumn leaves slowly fall,
And winter moves in.
Snow lies in the wood and the fields.
Oh how beautiful then is this world!
The snow, snow, snow, snow
Let's waltz and dance!
You with me. Me with you!
The snow, snow, snow, snow
Let's waltz and dance!
And from now on I'll always belong to you!

Mein Geburtstag *My Birthday*
10. Conversation
When is your birthday?
It is on the 19th of August!

Song First. Second. Third.
First, second, third, fourth.
Fifth, sixth, seventh, eighth.
Ninth, tenth, eleventh, twelfth.
When is your birthday?
The 21st of June,
Or the 30th of June?
The 31st of July?
When is your birthday?
Thirteenth, fourteenth?
Sixteenth, seventeenth?
Nineteenth, twentieth?
When is your birthday?

11. Song Happy Birthday!
Good luck on your birthday, dear Dietrich!
Good luck on your birthday, dear Anna!

Tiere *Animals*
12. Conversation
Have you got a pet?
Yes, I have a dog.
Oh yes! What is he called?
He's called Max.
What colour is he?
He is white.
How old is he?
He is nine.
Have you got a pet?
No I don't have a pet.
What a shame!

Rap Do you have a pet?
Do you have a pet, my good friend?
Yes, I have a pet, my good friend.
I have a cat. I have a snake.
I have a rat and also a mouse!
I have a goldfish. I have a hamster.
I have a bird and also a dog!
Do you have a pet, my good friend?
No, I don't have one!
What a shame, my friend!

13. Conversation
What animals do you find in the zoo?
You can find tigers and pandas in the zoo.
Oh! What colours are they?
The tiger is black and orange and the panda is black and white.

Copyright Carole Nicoll 2005

CD 1 Auf Englisch! In English!

Tiere *Animals (continued)*

Song The Zoo
E I O We are going to the zoo.
There is so much to see,
Tigers and peacocks.

E I AU The elephant is grey!
The adder disappears quickly.
The polar bear has white fur.

E I EU Camels eat hay.
The dolphin likes fish.
Parrots like nuts.

E I AI Very hungry is the shark.
Thorny is the porcupine.
The crocodile looks angry!

E I OCH Giraffes are very tall.
The panda stays in his house.
The pelican flies high above.

E I Q The kangaroo springs far.
The monkey grabs bananas.
The zebra has black and white stripes.

E I Z The seal is cheeky.
The lion comes from Africa.
The toucan from America.

E I O Today we were in the zoo.
There was so much to see.
Tigers and peacocks.

14. *Folksong Fox, you have stolen the goose!*
Fox! You have stolen the goose!
Bring it back! Bring it back!
Or the hunter will catch you
with his gun.
His big, long shotgun
will shoot pellets into you
these will colour you red
and then you are dead!
Dear little fox, some advice!
Don't be so stupid!
Come on, you don't need to have
a roast goose and mouse dinner!

15. *Rhyme & Folksong   All my ducks.*
All my ducks are swimming on the sea.
Their heads in the water. Their tails up.

Die Zeit *Time*
16. *Conversation*
Hello. What is the time, please?
It is eight o'clock.

Song What is the time?
Hello. What is the time, please?
It is midday.
Good evening. What is the time, please?
It is nineteen hundred hours.
Hello. What is the time, please?
Midnight.
Half eight. Five past eight. A quarter to eight.
A quarter past eight.
Ten past eight and ten past nine
Hello. What is the time?

17. *Rhyme and Folksong Big clocks.*
Big clocks go tick tock tick tock
Small clocks go ticketock ticketock
Tiny clocks go ticketocketicketocketick!

Sportarten *Sports*
18. *Conversation*
What is your favourite sport?
Football!
What sport don't you like?
I don't like bowling.
What sport do you hate?
I hate golf!

Rap Sports
What sport do you like best?
Tennis, rugby, hockey, swimming?
Snowboarding, bike riding or canoeing?
I don't like golf!!
What sport do you like best?
Sailing, running, boxing, riding?
Skateboarding or skating?
I love wrestling!
I prefer squash and judo.
I love fishing and football.
I like athletics.
I hate gymnastics!

Alphabet *Alphabet*
19. *Conversation*
What are you called?
I am called Dieter.
How do you spell that?
It is D. I. E. T. E. R.

Song ABC
A B C D E F G
H I J K L M N O P
Q R S T U V W
X Y Z

Monate *Months*
20. *Conversation*
When is your birthday?
My birthday is on the 19th of August.

Song January. February. March.
January. February. March. April. May.
June. July. August.
September. October. November. December.
June. July. August.

Die Stadt *The Town*
21. *Conversation*
Excuse me! How do I get to the bank?
Go right, then go left and then go straight on.
Thanks! Bye!

Song How do I get to the bank?
How do I get to the bank, please?
Go to the right, then go to the left,
Then go straight on and there it is!
Thank you !
How do I get to the post office, please?
How do I get to the market, please?
How do I get to the park, please?

Zahlen 1-20 *Numbers 1-20*
22. *Conversation*
Hello. How old are you?
I'm thirteen, and you?
I'm fourteen.
How old is he?
He is nine.
How old is she?
She is two!
Oh isn't she sweet?
Yes! See you tomorrow!

Song One Two Three
One, two, three.
Four, five, six.
Seven, eight, nine and ten.
Eleven and twelve. Eleven and twelve.
X2
Thirteen, fourteen.
Fifteen, sixteen.
Seventeen, eighteen
Nineteen, twenty.
X2

23. *Rhyme One, Two, Policemen*
One, two. Policemen!
Three, four. Officers!
Five, six. Old witch!
Seven, eight. Good night!
Nine, ten. Goodbye!

Farben *Colours*
24. *Conversation*
What colour is this?
It is pink. It is orange.
What are the colours of the German flag?
Black, red, gold, of course!

Song What colour is this?
What colour, what colour, what colour is this?
Red, yellow, green and blue.
Black, white, pink, brown.
Orange, violet, grey.
Silver, gold, light blue.

Weihnachten *Christmas*
25. *Conversation*
Merry Christmas and Happy New Year!

Scottish Folksong Auld Lang Syne.
Should auld acquaintance be forgot
And never brought to mind?
Should auld acquaintance be forgot
And days of auld lang syne?
For auld lang syne, my dear,
For auld lang syne,
We'll take a cup o' kindness yet
For auld lang syne.

Copyright Carole Nicoll 2005

CD 2 Auf Englisch! In English!

Grüße *Greetings*
1. Conversation 1.
Hello, how are you?
I'm fine thanks, and you?
Very well, thanks!
Goodbye, Mr Brown!
See you later, Mr Smith.
See you next week!

Conversation 2.
How are you?
Not very good!
Why?
I've got a sore finger!
Oh! What a shame!

2. Song Good Night Girl
Good night, girl!
Bye, Mr Small! (x2)
Hello, how are you?
I'm fine!
Good night, girl!
Bye, Mr Small!
Good-day, my boy!
What is your name? (x2)
I'm called Peter
And he's called Dieter!
Good-day, my boy.
What are you called?
Have a good weekend, and have fun!
Until next week, Mrs Glass!
Have a good journey, Peter!
Bye, and see you later!
Until early tomorrow morning and cheerio!

3. Conversation 3
See you later!
See you soon!
See you tonight!
See you tomorrow!
See you early tomorrow!
See you on Monday!
See you on Tuesday!
See you next week!
Have a good weekend!
Have a good holiday!
Have a good journey!
Goodbye!
Bye Bye!
Cheerio!
Sleep well!

Der Körper *The Body*
4. Song. Hans Says. (Simon Says)
Hans says. 'Show me your head!
And your nose too!'
Hans says. 'Show me your mouth
And your ears too!'
Hans says. 'Show me your hand
And your eyes too!'
Hans says. 'Show me your forehead at once
And your hair too!
Hans says. 'show me your chin
And your finger too!'
Hans says. 'Show me your knee
And your back too!'
Hans says. 'show me your heart
And your arms too!'
Hans says. 'Show me your leg at once
And your feet too!'

5. Folksong Little Brother
Little brother, come and dance with me,
I stretch both hands out to you!
Once here, once there,
Little brother, it is not difficult!

With the hands, clap, clap, clap!
With the feet, trip, trip, trap!
Once here, once there,
Little brother, it is not difficult!

With the little head, nick, nick, nick!
With the little finger, tick, tick, tick!
With the ears, hear, hear, hear!
With the nose, sniff, sniff, sniff!
With the legs, jump, jump, jump!
With the knees, bend, bend, bend!

Die Kleidung *Clothes*
6. Folksong My Hat.
My hat has got three corners.
Three corners has my hat.
And if it didn't have three corners.
It wouldn't be my hat!

7. Conversation.
What are you wearing?
A green pullover.
What are you wearing?
Some black trousers.
Describe your school uniform.
I'm wearing green trousers, a blue blazer
and a black and yellow tie.
Ah! How ghastly!

Song The Washing Machine.
What is in the washing machine?
A green skirt, a green skirt!
What is in the washing machine?
Granny's green skirt.

A yellow dress.
A red shawl.
A blue hat.
Smelly socks!

8. Folksong 'Show your feet'
Show your feet. Show your shoes,
And watch the busy washer women!
They wash, they wash, they wash all day long!
They wash, they wash, they wash all day long!
They iron, they iron, they iron all day long!
They iron, they iron, they iron all day long!

9. Rhyme The stork.
One, two, three, four, five.
The stork has red tights.
The frog doesn't have a house
And you are out!

10. Folksong
The Toadstool and the Mushroom
A little man is standing in the wood,
Very still, not saying a word.
He has a cloak of crimson.
Tell me, who might this little man be?
Who is standing in the woods all alone?
Wearing his little red cloak?

The little man is standing in the woods on one leg.
On his head he is wearing
A little black cap.
Tell me, who might this little man be?
Who is standing in the woods all alone,
With his little black cap?

Wie siehst du aus? *What do you look like?*
11. Conversation
What do you look like?
I have short, straight, black hair.
And you? What do you look like?
I have blue eyes!
And you over there?
I'm very big and kind!
And you?
I wear glasses!

Song What do you look like?
What do you look like?(x 5)
I have black hair.
I have blond hair.
I have red hair.
I have brown hair.

What do you look like?(x 5)
I have long hair.
I have short hair.
I have straight hair.
I have curly hair.

What do you look like?(x 5)
I have blue eyes.
I have green eyes.
I have grey eyes.
I have brown eyes.

What do you look like? (x 5)
I am very big.
I am very small.
I wear glasses.
I am very kind!

12. Folksong Skinny Hansel and Fatty Maid.
Skinny Hansel and Fatty Noodle Maid,
Let's go into the garden!
Let's shake the pears from the trees.
I'll shake off the big ones,
You shake off the small ones.
When the bag is full
We'll go home!
Don't run so fast and crazy, Skinny Hans!
I'm losing the pears and my shoes!
But you are only carrying the small one, Fatty Maid,
And I'm carrying the heavy bag with the big pears!

13. Tongue Twister The Gnomes.
Under the dense roots of the fir tree….
we can hear the gnomes fart!

Copyright Carole Nicoll 2005

CD 2 Auf Englisch! In English!

Die Familie *The Family*
14. Conversation
Have you any brothers or sisters?
Yes, I have a brother and a sister.
What is your brother called?
He is called Peter.
What is your sister called?
She is called Eva.
How old is she?
She is twelve.

Song Brother. Father. Grandfather.
Brother, father, grandfather.
Sister, mother, grandmother.
Aunt, uncle, cousins.
Nephew and step-brother.

Have you any brothers or sisters, Hans?
Yes, I have a brother.
Have you any brothers or sisters, Jens?
Yes, I have a sister.
A little dog.
A little cat.
Rabbits and
Guinea pigs.
Have you any brothers or sisters, child?
No, I'm an only child!

15. Rhyme & Folksong
There was a mother
Who had four children
Spring, Summer, Autumn and Winter.
Spring brought her flowers.
Summer brought her clover.
Autumn brought her grapes,
And Winter brought her snow.

Verkehrsmittel *Means of Transport*
16. Conversation
How do you get to school?
I go by car.
How do you get to school?
I go by bus, but sometimes I walk!
I also take the train from time to time.
Do you ever go to school in a flying saucer?
In a flying saucer? Never!

Song The tyres on the bus.
The tyres on the bus go
squelch, squelch, squelch (x3)
The tyres on the bus go
squelch, squelch, squelch (x3)
 All day long!

The engine on the bus goes
brumm, brumm, brumm. (x3)
The engine on the bus goes
brumm, brumm, brumm.
 All day long!

17. Song My Granny rides a motorbike!
My granny rides a motorbike in the chicken run!
Motorbike! Motorbike!
My granny rides a motorbike in the chicken run!
My granny is a very modern woman!

My granny has a radio in a hole in her tooth!....
My granny has a potty that lights up!......
My granny has curtains on her glasses!....

18. Folksong Tell me what the sailors are doing?
Tell me what the sailors are doing?
Norwegians, Germans and French.
When the waves in the sea are tossing.
Early in the morning.
Ho-He, and raise the sails!
Early in the morning!

They would love to wave to the girls,
Drink rum, or schnapps or whisky,
Rather than drown in the sea!
Early in the morning!
Ho-He, and raise the glasses!
Early in the morning!

Folksong My Bonnie
My Bonnie is far from home.
My Bonnie is far away on the sea.
You winds and waving waters,
Bring him back to me!
Bring back, bring back,
Oh bring him back to me! (x2)

Farben *Colours*
20. Conversation
What is your favourite colour?
My favourite colour is black.
What are your favourite colours?
My favourite colours are black and white!

Song Favourite Colour
What is your favourite colour, Hans?
Black, violet, brown?
Red, yellow, white, blue?
What is your favourite colour, Hans?
Violet, orange or light blue?

My favourite colour is surely red,
My favourite colour is surely pink,
My favourite colour is surely yellow,
My favourite colour is surely blue!

21. Rhyme At the Traffic Lights.
When it is red you must stop.
When it is green, you can go!
Have a good journey!

Song What is yellow?
What is yellow? (x2)
Do you know? (x2)
Bananas and lemons! (x2)
Sunshine! Sunshine!
What is green? (x2)
Do you know? (x2)
 Grass and apples! (x2)
 Grapes too! (X2)
 What is red? (x2)
 Do you know? (x2)
 Cherries and tomatoes! (X2)
 Strawberries too! (x2)

22. Rhyme The grass is green.
The grass is green.
The sea is blue.
The sand is yellow.
The mouse is grey.
The bear is brown.
The rose red.
Coal is black and
bread is white!

Folksong Green, green, green.
Green, green, green,
Are all my clothes!
Green, green, green,
Is all that I have!
I love, therefore, everything that is green,
Because my loved one is a hunter!

Blue. Sailor.
White. Baker.
Black. Chimney sweep.
Red. Fireman.
Multicoloured. Artist.

Das Alphabet *The Alphabet*
23. Vowel and Half vowel Rap.
A E I O U ..Y

24. Rhyme A B C D E
A B C D E
My head hurts!
F G H I K
The doctor is already here!
L M N O
Now I am happy!
P Q R S T
I'm better again. Yippee!
U V W X
Now nothing is missing!
Yes! 'J' is missing!
Y Z
Now I'm going to bed!

Folksong ABC 'The cat ran around in the snow!'
A B C! The cat ran around in the snow!
And when she came back in,
She had white boots on!
Oh dear! Oh dear!
The cat ran around in the snow!

Copyright Carole Nicoll 2005

CD 3 Auf Englisch! In English!

Weihnachten *Christmas*
25. Folksong We are going to Jerusalem!
We are going to Jerusalem,
And who is coming with us?
It isn't far from Bethlehem.
And you are coming with us!

26. Christmas Carol Silent Night
Still the night, holy the night.
All is calm all is bright.
Only the holiest of couples!
The beloved curly-haired boy.
Sleep in heavenly peace!
Sleep in heavenly peace!

Still the night, holy the night.
Shepherds are the first to learn
From the angel. Hallelujah!
Telling the news loudly from far and near,
Christ the Leader is here!
Christ the Leader is here!

27. Folksong Lantern! Lantern!
Lantern! Lantern!
Sun, moon and stars!
Burn brightly my candle! (x2)
But not my lovely lantern!

28. Christmas Carol Oh Christmas Tree!
Oh Christmas Tree! Oh Christmas Tree!
How green your leaves are! (x 2)
You are not only green in the summer time,
No, also in Winter when it is snowing!
Oh Christmas Tree! Oh Christmas Tree!
How green your leaves are!

Oh Christmas Tree! Oh Christmas Tree!
I like you very much! (x 2)
How often at Christmas time,
Has a tree of your kind given me joy!
Oh Christmas Tree, Oh Christmas Tree!
I like you very much!

Im Klassenzimmer *In the Classroom*
29. Conversation
What have you got in your rucksack?
In my rucksack I have a book, a jotter,
a calendar and a calculator.
What is there in the classroom?
In the classroom there are chairs, tables,
a teacher and a rubbish bin!

30. Song From the blue mountains.
We are from the blue mountains,
Our teacher is just as stupid as we are!
With his finger in his nose,
He looks like an Easter Bunny!
We are from the blue mountains!

Café *Café*
31. Rhyme No wine.
'No wine!' said the pig!
'Where shall we dance?'
said the bugs.
'In the house!' said the mouse.
'On the table!' said the fish!

(Not on a CD)
Rhyme
My wish is small
but it is true
stay really healthy
in the New Year!

Copyright Carole Nicoll 2005

CD 3 Auf Englisch! In English!

Jahreszeiten Seasons
1. Conversation
The autumn, the winter,
The spring, the summer!
In which season is your birthday?
My birthday is in spring!
What is the weather like in spring?
Its fine, but it rains.
What is your favourite season?
My favourite season is autumn.
Why?
I love wind and clouds!
Really?

2. Folksong Buzz, buzz, buzz!
Buzz, buzz, buzz,
Little bee buzz around!
Look in flowers,
Look in little flowers,
Get a little drop,
Get a little crumb!
Buzz, buzz, buzz,
Little bee buzz around!

3. Folksong Cuckoo
Cuckoo! Cuckoo!
Calls in the wood.
Let us sing dance and jump!
Spring! Spring!
Will soon be here!

4. Folksong All the birds are already here!
All the birds are already here!
All the birds, all of them!
Blackbirds, thrush, finch and starling
And the whole flock of birds,
Wish you a happy year,
Good health and God's blessing!

5. Rhyme Yellow leaf. Fall off.
Yellow leaf,
Fall off,
Until the tree,
Has no more leaves left!

Red leaf,
Fall off,
Until the tree,
Has no more leaves left!

Multicoloured leaf,
Fall off,
Until the tree,
Has no more leaves left!

6. Folksong Yes! Summertime is here!
Yes, yes, yes! Summertime is here!
We want to go in the garden.
We don't want to wait anymore!
Yes, yes, yes. The summertime is here!

Yes, yes, yes! The summertime is here!
Summer has won! Winter has lost!
Yes, yes, yes! Summertime is here!

7. Rhyme Ru Ru Risch.
Ru ru risch,
In winter it is cold,
The nightingale sings in the summer.
All the birds rejoice!
Ru ru risch,
In winter it is cold!

Mein Geburtstag My Birthday
8. Conversation
All the best on your birthday!
Yes! All the best!
What did you get for your birthday?
I got a mobile phone!
Oh! Cool!

Song Those who are born in January
Those who are born in January,
Get up! Get up! Get up!
In Febrary….
In March …………..…..
In April…..
In May
and so on……

Der Bauernhof The Farm
9. Song Hop! Hop! Hop!
Hop!, hop!, hop!
Little pony gallops!
Over tree stumps and stones,
But don't break your legs!
Hop, hop, hop, hop, hop!
Little pony gallops!

10. Tongue Twister Swim, Swan, Swim!
Swim, Swan, Swim!
Swan as white as snow!
Swim, Swan, Swim!
Swim over the sea!

11. Old Scottish Folksong.
Old MacDonald had a farm
Old MacDonald had a house!
Ee ay ee ay oh!
A dog looked out of the window!
Ee ay ee ay oh!
With a woof woof here
And a woof woof there
Here a woof, there a woof
Everywhere a woof woof!
Old MacDonald had a house!
Ee ay ee ay oh!

A horse looked out of the window!
Neigh! Neigh!
A mouse looked out of the window!
Squeak! Squeak!
A cow looked out of the window!!
Moo! Moo!
A hen looked out of the window!
Cackle! Cackle!
A pig looked out of the window!
Snort! Snort!

12.Tongue Twister Fisherman Fritz!
Fisherman Fritz catches fresh fish.

13. Folksong Little bunny sitting in his burrow.
Little bunny is sitting in his burrow fast asleep!
Are you ill, little bunny?
Can't you hop around anymore?
Hop, bunny! Hop, bunny! Hop, bunny!

Little bunny, mind that dog!
He has sharp teeth,
That he could bury into you!
Hop, bunny! Hop, bunny! Hop, bunny!

14. Rhyme A little shrew.
A little shrew,
Ran around the town hall,
He wanted to buy himself something,
But got lost!

Folksong Widewidewenne
My turkey is called 'Widewidewenne'!
My chicken is called 'Can't Rest'!
My goose is called 'Wiggly Tail'!
My goat is called 'Black and White'!
My pig is called 'Short Legs'!
My turkey is called 'Widewidewenne'!

15. Rhyme
If the chickens are as flat as a plate,
Then the tractor was faster than them again!

16. Folksong 'The cuckoo and the donkey'
The cuckoo and the donkey had a quarrel.
Who could sing better,
In the month of May.

The cuckoo said 'I can'
And started to shout!
'I can do it better'
The donkey joined in.

That sounded so lovely and sweet,
So lovely from far and near.
They both sang together…
'Cuckoo, cuckoo', 'Ee aw, ee aw!'

Das Wetter The Weather
17. Conversation
What is the weather like today?
Today it is bad.
What is the weather like in autumn?
In autumn it is windy and bad!
What is the weather like in winter?
In winter it is cold and it is snowing!
What is the weather like in spring?
In spring it rains.
What is the weather like in summer?
In summer it is hot and sunny.
What is the weather like in Scotland?
In Scotland! Oh! It is often foggy and always cloudy!

Copyright Carole Nicoll 2005

CD 3 Auf Englisch! In English!

Das Wetter (continued)
18. Rhyme When the sun shines.
When the sun shines,
The sky is clear.
When the rain comes,
The clouds are there!

Folksong It is raining!
It is raining! It is raining!
It will rain until it stops!
And when it has rained enough,
Then it will stop!

19. Rhyme Incy Wincy Spider
Incy Wincy Spider
How long your thread is!
The rain comes down,
And your thread breaks!
Then comes the sun,
And dries up the rain.
Incy Wincy Spider
Clambers back up again!

20. Rhyme Snowflakes.
Little snowflakes!
Little white rocks!
Come down into the valley!
Then we'll build a snowman,
And throw snowballs!

Der Zoo Zoo
21. Conversation
What is your favourite zoo animal?
My favourite zoo animal is the elephant!
Why?
Because he is big and strong but also very friendly!
What are your favourite animals in the zoo?
My favourite animals are seals and monkeys.
Why?
Because they are so funny!

22. Joke The Elephant.
What is the difference between an African elephant and an Asian Elephant?
I don't know!
10,000 kilometres!

23. Tongue Twister Ten goats.
Ten goats pulls 10 x 100 grams of sugar to the zoo!

Die Zeit *The Time*
24. Conversation Daily Routine
When do you leave the house?
I leave the house at 7o'clock.
When do you have lunch?
I have lunch at one o'clock.
When do you come back home?
I come back home at four o'clock.
When do you have dinner?
I have dinner at seven o'clock.
When do you go to bed?
I go to bed at ten o'clock.

25. Rhyme
Early every morning at six
The little witch arrives.
Early every morning at seven
She peels carrots.
Early every morning at eight
She makes coffee.
Early every morning at nine
She goes into the barn.
Early every morning at ten
She carries wood and twigs.
She makes a fire at eleven
And cooks until twelve.
Frogs' legs and crab and fish.
Quick, children, come to the table!

Sportarten *Sports*
26. Conversation.
What is your favourite sport?
Cycling! And you?
I prefer ice skating!
Why?
It is fun and difficult!

Die Stadt *The Town*
27. Conversation.
Where do you live?
I live in Aberdeen in North Scotland.
Is Aberdeen a town or a village?
It is a town.
What is there to do in Aberdeen?
There is a skating rink, a sports centre and lots of shops.
That is just great!

28. French Folksong Avignon Bridge.
On the bridge at Avignon,
Let's dance! Let's dance!
On the bridge at Avignon,
Let's dance round and round!

29. English Folksong London Bridge.
London Bridge has a hole,
Has a hole! Has a hole!
By the hole still stands
My Lady!

Zahlen *Numbers*
30. Conversation 1
Hey! Volker! What is your phone number?
My number? 70 61 73.
And you Peter?
My number is 70 76 81.
Telephone for me!
No, for me!

31. Conversation 2
What is this?
This is thirty.
What is this?
This is sixty!
What is one and five?
One and five is six.
What is ten minus one?
Ten minus one is nine!
What is two times two?
Two times two is four.
And ten divided by two?
Ten divided by two is five.

32. Joke Eight Legs.
What has eight legs, two wheels and goes really fast?
I don't know!
A spider on a motorbike!

In meinem Schlafzimmer *In My Bedroom*
33. Conversation.
What is your room like?
It is quite small!
What do you have in your room?
In my room I have a shelf,
A big bed and a TV!
A TV! You are lucky!

Lullaby Sleep, little child, sleep
Sleep, little child, sleep!
Your father is minding sheep!
Mother is shaking the little tree,
A small dream tumbles down
Sleep, little child, sleep!

Lullaby Big, Brown Beetle Fly Away
Big, brown beetle, fly away!
Your father is at war!
Your mother is in Pommerland, (old Poland)
Pommerland is all burnt down!
Fly away big, brown beetle!

Copyright Carole Nicoll 2005

Acknowledgements

Acknowledgements
The author would like to thank the following establishments and individuals for their help and support during the production of Deutsch! Deutsch!.

Pupils from Aberdeen Grammar School
Carla and Anna Plasberg Hill.
Dietrich and Morag Leopoldt.
Ilka Reglitz.

Pupils from *Cults Academy, Aberdeen*
Dominic and Daniel O'Riordan.

Pupils from *The Dutch School, Aberdeen*
Janna and Sophie Stammeijer.

Pupils from *The Total French School, Aberdeen*
Richard and Robert Heithorst.

Pupils from *Robert Gordon's College, Aberdeen*
Isla Mackenzie and Natasha Sinclair.

Parents and Teachers
Ulrike Plasberg Hill, German Specialist *(ASG)* Associated School Groups Aberdeen
Mika Mackenzie, *D.I.A. Deutsche in Aberdeen. (Aberdeen German Community)*
Joyce Tease, Head of *Modern Languages Aberdeen Grammar School.*
Kerry Joss and Marilyn Lowden, *Robert Gordon's College, Aberdeen.*
Liza Russell, Ulrike Stammeijer, Ingrid O'Riordan, Suzanne Heithorst.

Music and Sound Mixing
Niall Mathewson.

ICT advisors
Daphne Parlour and Stefan Mallia.

Proof Advisors
Moira Edmunds, Education Development Service, Angus Council.
Urs Dornbierer, Switzerland. Till Techatscheck, Goethe Institute.

Printing
The Team at X. I .C.

Colleagues, friends and acquaintances who have inspired me, and whose support has been appreciated.
Elizabeth Anderson, *Aberdeen City*.
Mary Farries, Sylvie Grigas, Pat Richard, Graham Bowman and Tom Cumming.

Dedicated to my husband Alan and my children Lucy, Jack, Andrew, Kirsty and Max (our dog).

Carole Nicoll, **Project co-ordinator**. October 2005 © The Language Factory.

Copyright Carole Nicoll 2005